A
GOOMBA'S
Guide to Life

RICK DUFRESNE
(PLEASE RETURN)

A GOOMBA'S
Guide to Life

STEVEN R. SCHIRRIPA

and

Charles Fleming

THREE RIVERS PRESS
NEW YORK

Published by Three Rivers Press, New York, New York.
Member of the Crown Publishing Group, a division of Random House, Inc.
www.randomhouse.com

THREE RIVERS PRESS and the tugboat design are registered trademarks
of Random House, Inc.

Originally published in hardcover by Clarkson Potter/Publishers, a division of
Random House, Inc., in 2002.

Printed in the United States of America

Design by Maggie Hinders

Library of Congress Cataloging-in-Publication Data
Schirripa, Steven R.
A goomba's guide to life / by Steven R. Schirripa and Charles Fleming.
1st ed.
1. Italian Americans—Humor. I. Fleming, Charles. II. Title.
PN6231.I85 S35 2002

814'.6—dc21   2002012218
ISBN 1-4000-5081-2

10 9 8 7 6 5 4 3 2 1

First Paperback Edition

To Laura, Bria, and Ciara

and to three goomba heroes, Joey, Carl, and Louie.

ACKNOWLEDGMENTS

Steve Schirripa would like to thank, for their invaluable help in making this book possible, Bernie Allen, Louie Anderson, Frank Anobile Sr. and Frank Anobile Jr., Mike Anobile Jr., Dave Becky, Pat Bolino, Mitchell Burgess, John Capotonto, David Chase, Dominic Chianese, Diane Costello, Michael De Georgio, Nick Di Paolo, Carmine Esposito Sr., Carmine Esposito Jr., Ray Favero, Bob Fiandra, Hugh Fink, Robert Funaro, James Gandolfini, Joseph R. Gannascoli, Laurie Gomez, Robin Green, Roger Haber, Mike Hernandez, Mike Harriot, Richie and Anthony Iocolano, Kevin James, Pam Krauss, everyone at La Bella Ferrara, Ilene Landress, Don Learned, Jim and Jane Lemos, Bill Maher, Scott Manners, Joe Marzella, Guido Maurino, Cheryl McLean, Charlie Melfi, Jerry Miner, Vinnie Montalto, Charles Najjar, Joe Pantoliano, Lisa Perkins, Jimmie Raya, Willie Rizzo, Chris Rock, Rocky from Mulberry Street, Ray Romano, Rory Rosegarten, Richard Scanlon, Lorraine Schirripa,

Ralph Schirripa, Jeff Singer, Tony Sirico, Tim Stone, Jeff Sussman, Bob Vannucci, Steven Van Zandt, John Ventimiglia, David Vigliano, Patricia Weber, Bill Westerman, Terry Winter, Premiere Caterers, Il Cortile Restaurant, all his friends at the Riviera Hotel and Casino, the entire cast and crew of *The Sopranos,* all his friends back in Bensonhurst, and his wife, Laura, and daughters, Ciara and Bria.

Charles Fleming would like to thank David Vigliano, Pam Krauss, and his wife, Julie Singer, and daughters, Katherine and Frances.

CONTENTS

INTRODUCTION

Welcome to the world of goomba. This is your guide. What we got here is two things. First is the story of me, Steve Schirripa, and why I'm proud to be a goomba. Second is the story of what a goomba is, and what it means to be one.

This ain't as easy as it looks. The first part—no problem. I know exactly how I was raised, and how I went from a Bensonhurst kid to a guy with a big job at one of the biggest casinos in Las Vegas to a man with a wife and two kids and a regular berth on one of the best television shows that ever was, *The Sopranos*.

The second part—that's more difficult. Explaining and defining the goomba isn't easy. It *looks* easy. How hard could it be? Everyone knows what a goomba is, right? He's a fat Italian jerk, right, or a gangster?

Wrong. That ain't the goomba. The goomba is more complicated than that.

With this book, I'm going to try to explain what the goomba is, what the goomba isn't, what the

My 1st communion. A big day for any goomba.

goomba does, how he does it, and how an ordinary non-goomba could take a tip or two and learn to live life a little better.

Now, maybe you're wondering why would anyone want to be a goomba. It's an insult, right? Not necessarily. To most goombas, the word "goomba" is a term of endearment. He's what the Jews would call a *mensch,* or what a Southerner calls a "good ol' boy." A goomba is a man's man. He's tough. He's usually pretty big. He's got a big appetite, too—for food, and booze, and broads, most of the time.

He's not too smart, maybe, and probably not too educated. He ain't no rocket scientist, and he ain't working on Wall Street. He might not have a lot to say. But he ain't stupid, either. Like my friend Vinnie says, "When a fish opens his mouth, he gets hooked." The goomba knows when to keep his mouth shut.

When he does talk, he's funny and full of life. He speaks what's on his mind. He tells the truth—except to his wife or the cops. He ain't no phony—what you see is what you get. The goomba doesn't explain, and the goomba doesn't complain.

The goomba treats everyone alike. This is another key element to the goomba character. The true goomba is very comfortable being who he is. So, he ain't kissing nobody's ass just to feel better about himself, and he ain't bullying anybody either. He might be a big guy, but you won't find him pushing around any little guys. Whether he's talking to a senator or a sanitation worker, he's gonna be straight and solid. He's gonna tip the maitre d' to get a good table, but he's gonna duke the kid at the car wash, too, just to show his appreciation. He is just as polite to the priest that says the Mass at his church as he is to the waitress who serves the spaghetti at his local *trattoria*. And he'll say "thank you" or "fuck you" to either one of them, depending on the situation.

Above all else, the goomba is very loyal. He will never betray his family or his friends. He'd die first. You can depend on the goomba to stand up for himself and for his friends, to the end. For this reason, you wouldn't want to pick a fight with a goomba unless you got more friends around than he has. If at all possible, you don't want to go up against a goomba in a fight. You want the goomba *behind* you in a fight.

~ ~ ~

IF I LIKE a guy, I might say, "He's okay. He's a real goomba." If he does something funny, or foolish, I might say, "What a goomba!" If I want to describe a certain kind of guy from the neighborhood, one of a hundred guys that I grew up with and I'm still friends with, there is no other word to use. The guy's a goomba. What's he like? He's a real goomba.

Which still doesn't explain it. You *can't* explain it.

I was a guest on a game show recently. We were rehearsing. It was going great. We were laughing and joking and having fun, until the producer came out. He looked worried. He said, "Steve, could you do me a favor? Could you try to be a little more . . . a little more . . . you know . . ."

I said, "You want me to *goomba* it up a little?"

And he said, "Yes! Could you do that?"

He wanted more of a certain kind of attitude. And maybe that's what goomba really is. It's a certain kind of attitude.

And I gotta tell you something: I have gone a long way on attitude. Or I should say the goomba attitude has helped me get where I got in my life. Attitude, plus some persistence and some good luck and lots of hard work. But first, attitude.

~ ~ ~

I WAS A young goomba, working in Las Vegas as a maitre d', when I heard that the film director Martin Scorsese was coming to town to make a movie called *Casino*. A friend suggested I go and audition. The casting director was looking for a local guy to play the maitre d' at a casino. My friend said, "You *are* a maitre d' at a casino. You're a natural!"

So I went up for the job. I didn't have any business doing this. I had never acted in a movie. I had only done a few small TV things. I had no idea what an actor did. I had no idea what a director expected, or what a casting director was looking for. But I went up for the job anyway. What could I lose?

I lost the job, is what I lost. Or I didn't get it, anyway. Whatever the casting director thought a maitre d' at a casino was—it wasn't me. But I stuck around, and I got cast in another role, a smaller one. For one day's work, working with Robert De Niro and Joe Pesci, I got my union card for the Screen Actors Guild. After that I started going out for all kinds of acting jobs. I kept my day job, too, but I started looking for work as an actor.

In the meantime, my day job changed. I was promoted from maitre d' to entertainment director at The Riviera Hotel and Casino. My main job was booking entertainment for the hotel, including the comedy club.

I started working pretty regularly as an actor, too.

Because I'm a big guy, and because I'm Italian, most of the parts were for wise guys. Tough guys. Bad guys. Heavies. Goombas, in other words. I got goomba parts in *Fear and Loathing in Las Vegas* and *Play It to the Bone*. I got a part in *The Adventures of Joe Dirt* and in *The Flintstones: Viva Rock Vegas*. I was on TV, in *Chicago Hope* and *The King of Queens*. I worked pretty steady for a guy that wasn't an actor.

Most of those parts, it wasn't that hard to know how to play them. I'd been around wise guys my whole life—guys from my childhood, guys from the neighborhood, guys I used to see standing on the corner and in the restaurants. I'd been around all these tough guys in Vegas for years, too. I never went to any of them for research or anything, but I could have if I needed to. I mean, if I had to clip a guy, in a movie, I'd know where to go to learn how to do it.

Looking back, I see now that I got all that work done on the strength of attitude. It was that same attitude that got me the job on *The Sopranos*.

It could look kind of accidental. In fact, a couple of guys I know said to me, "How'd you luck into a job like that?" It wasn't luck. It was hard work, along with that attitude thing. It was goomba endurance.

~ ~ ~

So, you want a piece of that? Sure you do! Then start reading. The chapters that follow will show you how to spot a goomba, how to be a goomba, how to talk and dress and act like a goomba, and how to eat and cook like one, too. There's everything from goomba career counseling (the goomba doesn't make a good interior decorator) to goomba baby names (the goomba should call his son Rocco or Vito, not Jason or Hunter) to goomba relationships (if your girlfriend asks, "Does this dress make me look fat?" the goomba must answer, "No. It's your big ass that makes you look fat") to goomba dining (never expect real Italian food if the menu says "pasta" or "authentic" on it; real Italians say "macaroni" or "spaghetti," and they never say they're "authentic" unless they're not). There's lists of things you should do, and shouldn't do, and things you can say, and can never say. There's inside dope on how to get what you want, how to say what you want, how to be what you want and how to get people to treat you the way you want—all of the time, without knocking heads with everybody you meet.

If you pay attention and follow the lessons in these pages, you might not actually become a goomba, but you might start to feel a little like a goomba. And you'll certainly learn to live life a little better—the goomba way.

Chapter 1

GOOMBA 101

A goomba will never let
you pick up a check.
You're the guest.
He'll kill you before he'll
let you pay.

What's a goomba? Who's a goomba? What's the difference between a goomba and a gangster? What's the difference between a goomba and a regular Italian? Are there goombas in other countries? Is there any such thing as a Jewish goomba, or a black goomba, or an Episcopalian goomba?

Keep your shirt on. I'm gonna lay it out for you here. This is the lesson on goomba.

A goomba is a certain kind of Italian-American, probably born on the east coast—New York, New Jersey, Boston, Rhode Island—probably third generation from the old country. He's not a gangster. He's not a wise guy, or a made man, or a good fella, or a member of the Family—but he knows those guys, or guys like that, and some of them know him. He's Italian through and through, but he's a special kind of Italian-American hybrid. He's not old country Italian. There are no goombas in other countries, even Italy. There may be some kind of equivalent—some kind of tough guy from Iceland or Russia or somewhere—but the only true goomba is your Italian-American goomba.

You know the stereotype. It's the fat guy sitting at the corner social club, drinking espresso and playing cards and eating a big plate of soggy macaroni. He's got his napkin tucked into his collar. He's wearing a pair of baggy black pants, a pair of patent leather shoes, and one of those guinea shirts, the sleeveless T-shirts that some guys use as underwear. He has nine gold chains hanging from his neck. He's got pinky rings on all three pinkies. The look on his face says "Moron." This guy doesn't have a job, or maybe he's a petty criminal of some kind, because that's the only work he's smart enough to do. He's almost mobbed up. The only exercise he ever gets is maybe lifting some weights and hoisting that fork full of macaroni. If he talks, he only says something like, "What are you looking at?"

That's the cliché. And like every cliché, it's partly right. But I myself am a goomba—and I'm not *any* of that stuff. I'm a college graduate. I know how to read a book. I don't sit around all day playing cards and sucking garlic. I don't beat my wife. I've never been in jail. I don't play the ponies or the numbers. I have never taken out a contract on anyone. But I'm a goomba, right to the heart, and I'm proud of it.

Some Italians take offense if you call them a goomba. Especially if you say it the wrong way. It's kind of like how a black guy can use the "N" word to another black guy. Or how a black guy can call his friend "blood." Or how a certain kind of hillbilly can call someone a "redneck," or how a guy from the Midwest can call someone an "Okie." You say it with a smile, you might get a laugh. You say it any other way, or you say it and you're not an Okie or a redneck yourself . . . you're gonna get your clock cleaned.

The word "goomba" itself is a little confusing. No one knows where it really comes from. Most people think it started off as the word "compadre," which is a term of respect. You can use it to refer to your godfather, your protector, your older cousin or older brother or uncle. From "compadre," it got shortened to "compa," which got twisted into "gomba," which got turned into "goomba."

If this sounds a little far fetched, you should know right now that goombas do that with words. Everything gets chopped up, chopped down, and turned into a slang version of the original word. No goomba says "pasta e fagioli" when he means a soup made of noodles and beans. He says, "pasta fazool." No goomba says "mozzarella." It's always, "mozza-*rell*." No one says "proscuitto." It's just, "pro-*shoot*." Even English words get the treatment. No one says "one hundred dollars," when they mean $100. They may say a c-note or "a hundge." As in, "I gave the guy a c-note," or, "The guy's into me for two hundge." Even the word "wop" is supposed to be a short version of the Italian word "guapo," which means "handsome." It started as a compliment, but it got turned into an insult. Some people even said WOP stands for without papers, a reference to their recent immigrant status.

That has almost happened with the word "goomba." When used by non-goombas, it can be a derogatory word. Along with some of those other derogatory words that ignorant people sometimes use to describe the goomba.

Goomba is not "wop." It's not "guinea." It's not "dago." These terms are always offensive to an Italian-American, whether he's a goomba or not. They are words used by non-Italians to insult Italians. It is not smart to do this. You shouldn't use these words around a goomba unless you are a masochist and have excellent health insurance. Somebody's gonna get hurt, and it ain't gonna be the goomba. Better stick to "goomba," and better use it the right way.

There are no goombas in other cultures, either—not even other American cultures. There is no such thing as a Jewish goomba—though there is probably a Yiddish word that means something like goomba, one of those words that starts with a "sch" and sounds like you're trying to talk with a slab of prosciutto in your mouth—even though there are plenty of Jewish tough guys. There's no such thing as a Puerto Rican goomba, even though some of those guys are plenty tough, too. There's no black goombas. There's no WASP goombas.

So, you're asking yourself, "Am I a goomba?" If you have to ask, the answer is probably, "No." But here are some ways to tell.

A goomba will never back down from a fight, even if he's outnumbered or outmatched and he's about to get his ass kicked. A goomba will always stay in the fight until he can't fight any more. It's victory, or the hospital. There's no in-between.

A goomba will never let you pick up a check. You're the guest. He'll kill you before he'll let you pay.

A goomba will never let anyone insult his wife, his mother, or any other woman present. He's that kind of gentleman. You're risking your life if you push this.

A goomba will always drop anything he's doing if there's food around—as long as it's Italian food.

There's the old joke about a guy who got into a terrible car accident. He was thrown from the vehicle, and was lying in the street, bleeding, with broken bones. But the truck he'd run into was doing deliveries for an Italian deli. He's practically dying, but he looks up and says, "This prosciutto, it's imported? Delicious!"

Goombas all dress alike. No matter if they're from New York, or Detroit, or Philly, or Chicago, or Cleveland. They might sound different. But until they open their mouths, they all look like guys from the neighborhood.

The goomba is usually a big guy. He's wearing a jogging suit, and a pinky ring, and a gold watch and some gold chains around his neck. Or otherwise maybe he's wearing black see-through socks, and pointy black shoes, and shorts—on a hot summer day. Maybe he's wearing black pants and a guinea T-shirt, if he's a more old-fashioned goomba. The modern goomba, he wears the jogging suit during the day and the real suit at night. If it's daytime, he's dressed like he's trying to pick up chicks at the gym. If it's nighttime, he's dressed like he's trying to pick up chicks at a nightclub. It doesn't matter if you're going to meet the godfather or taking your kids out for an ice cream cone. This is the uniform.

You can also tell a goomba from the way he talks.

First of all, certain things you never say out loud. Sums of money, for example. You never say, "He owes me four thousand dollars." Never. You say, "He's into me four large."

Even the way guys talk in the movies, they never say what they mean. The gangsters use gangster slang. They never say, "That guy has a gun in his pocket." They say, "Be careful. He's dressed heavy." They don't talk about hurting people, either. They never say, "We killed him." Murder is a felony. They don't talk about that. They say "whacked" or "clipped" or "iced" or "aced" or "hit" or "burned" or "popped" or whatever.

But you can also know a goomba from the things he *doesn't* say. Here are some things you will never, ever hear a goomba say:

> Two tickets for *The Vagina Monologues*, please.
> Excellent putt, Arthur.
> Nathan Lane? I adore Nathan Lane.
> What this country needs is handgun control.
> Pass the mayonnaise, please.
> Snoop Dogg rocks.
> Guilty, your honor.

Lots of goomba lingo seems to be related to gangster lingo. You've heard guys on *The Sopranos* use this language. And guys in movies like *GoodFellas,* or *Casino,* or *Analyze This.* I'm not suggesting you talk this way, and I'm not saying the average goomba even needs to know this stuff. But it's a helpful glossary just in case you're confused about what you're hearing.

MOB SLANG, Part I

Bad-a-bing—multipurpose interjection, meaning anything from "That's that," to "Hallelujah," to "I'll take care of it," to "The guy is dead meat." See *fuhgeddaboudit.*

Break an egg—kill someone for professional reasons

Button—a "made" Mafia member; someone who can *break an egg*

Clip—See *break an egg*

Contract—verbal agreement to *break an egg*

Friend of mine—a member of the Mafia

Fuhgeddaboudit—multipurpose interjection, meaning anything from "You're welcome," to "Don't mention it," to "You have no idea," to "I'll take care of it," to "The guy is dead meat."

Hard-on—a tough guy; a grudge

Hard-on with a suitcase—a lawyer; a female lawyer is *half a hard-on with a suitcase*

Broken-down valise—a guy who's down on his luck

Broken ass—luck, as in, "He's got a broken ass," which means he's very lucky.

Hit—See break an egg

Ice—See break an egg

Juice—strength, pull, or power

EXAMPLE: "I'd gonna send over a friend of mine to break an egg on this hard-on with a suitcase who thinks he's got enough juice to hire his own buttons." This is just an example. A real tough guy would never say all that. He'd say, "I'll take care of it." And then you'd see something in the papers. Bad-a-bing.

Everybody who watches TV and the movies knows a few goomba expressions. Everyone knows how to say "fuhgeddaboudit." This is a very useful term, because it's very flexible. It can mean almost anything.

It means, "Don't mention it":
"Thanks for helping me out." "Fugheddaboudit."

It means, "You have no idea":
"Is she beautiful? Fugheddaboudit."

It means, "Don't get me started":
"Bad day at the track?"
"Fugheddaboudit."

And everyone knows all that Marlon Brando and Robert De Niro tough-guy stuff from *The Godfather* and *Taxi Driver*. Ask someone to imitate a wise guy, and chances are nine out of ten he'll say either "I made him an offer he couldn't refuse," or "You talkin' to *me*?"

Like any dialect, however, goombataliano is rich and varied. Certain words must be mastered before any real use can be made of the whole vocabulary.

The words "what" and "right," for example, are very important. They stress disagreement on the part of the speaker, or disbelief in what the speaker has just heard. For example:

"You should start saving now for your retirement."

"Right. Like I'm going to *have* a retirement."

Or:

"You should think about anger management classes."

"What? I only shot the guy once."

Or:

"I think we need to reach out to people of all ethnicities."

"Right. And I'm sleeping with Whitney Houston."

Similarly, words that in other cultures express pleasure or approval can, in goombataliano, express the opposite. Notice how "great" and "terrific" are used here.

"I got two tickets to *Showboat*."

"Great. Now everyone will know you're gay."

Or:

"Honey, I put a downpayment on that new refrigerator."

"Terrific. Now we can qualify for food stamps."

Insults in goombataliano are often delivered with subtlety, at the end of a sentence, through a peculiarly goomba formula in which the insult is bracketed by the word "you" or the more slangy "ya."

For example, "I oughta break your legs, you *mook* you." Or, "Come here, ya dope ya."

Similarly, an adjectival insult is often suspended at the end of a sentence, almost as an afterthought, following an observation about the person insulted.

"He's lying, the bastard." Or, "He's been skimming, the rat."

On the other hand, a real goomba would never, ever

say certain things. Here's another list of things a goomba will never, ever say:

> Do these briefs make my ass look fat?
> Don't get mad. Let's talk this out.
> Shakespeare? I prefer the sonnets to the plays.
> You go girl.
> Stop. I bruise easy.
> There's a white sale at Macy's.
> I like boxing, but the violence is a real turn-off.

Another way you can tell the goombas from the non-goombas is . . . volume. Goombas are kind of loud. They live life at a high level of enjoyment. They do things in dramatic ways. And they make a lot of noise doing it.

It's a cultural thing. People from other places don't get it. My wife is from Las Vegas, from a Mexican family. The first time I brought her home to meet my family, she said, "All the yelling and arguing. What are they always screaming about?"

I said, "Nothing. That's how they talk."

Goomba families, they're loud. They're loving and generous and big-hearted and nice. But loud. Always, they're loud.

It's not just language. You can tell a goomba from several other things, too. Favorite movies. Favorite music. Tastes in food, and sports. Hobbies. Here are a few tips.

GOOMBA CULTURE

GOOMBA CULTURE IS pretty simple stuff. All those clichés? They're true. If you're a real goomba, you really do listen to Frank Sinatra. This is the perfect music for every occasion. No matter what's happening, it sounds better if you're listening to Sinatra. It's not just because he's Italian, or because he's from the neighborhood, or because he's famous. It's because he's Frank. Nothing else sounds like Sinatra. It's like the goomba soundtrack.

You can also listen to Tony Bennett. Remember, his real name is Anthony Benedetto. He's real Italian, like Frank. You can always listen to Jerry Vale, who is one of the great entertainers—played Vegas, played the Catskills, wonderful singer. You can listen to Al Martino. You can listen to Connie Francis, who's also Italian. Real name: Concetta Franconero. You can never go wrong with Dean Martin—real name, Dino

Crocetti. You might want a little Louie Prima in there, definitely Jimmy Rosselli, just for fun. Maybe, you might throw in a little Barry White. I don't know where he fits in, but the goomba likes him.

But that's it. That's where goomba music stops.

There is no such thing as goomba rap. We don't listen to rap, ever. Or hip hop. There is no such thing as goomba bubble gum music. There is no goomba Britney Spears. There is no goomba Michael Jackson. Goomba music requires a horn section and a conductor, like something you'd see in a Vegas casino lounge. If it's got electric guitars, long hair, bare mid-sections, go-go dancers, a D.J. or dreadlocks . . . it ain't goomba music. If it's got a banjo . . . it ain't goomba music. If it's got a guy in a tuxedo, and a big microphone, and it sounds like it was arranged by Nelson Riddle—that's goomba music! Unless it's Harry Connick Jr., in which case it's sort of goomba lite.

Goomba movies are just as easy to identify. Everyone knows these movies. Every goomba with a VCR owns a copy of *The Godfather*. Every goomba has seen *GoodFellas* a hundred times. And *Mean Streets*. And *Raging Bull* and *Casino*. And *Scarface,* with Al Pacino. *Rocky*. Every goomba with cable TV watches *The Sopranos*. Of course.

MOB SLANG, Part II

Jammed up—sent to prison

Mobbed up—involved with LCN. A good thing.

Pinched—arrested. A bad thing.

Popped—see *pinched*

Program, the—the federal witness protection program

Rat—to cooperate with the police, name names, identify co-conspirators; or, the person who does these things

Sing—to rat

Sit-down—big meeting between fighting families

Skipper—the boss of a mob crew

Stand-up—dependable; used to describe a guy who won't rat

Squealer—see *rat*. See also *stool pigeon, stoolie, canary, snitch*, etc.

Swag—stolen goods

Whack—to kill

Wise guy—in Mafia terms, a made man, someone you cannot whack without special permission

> EXAMPLE: "Everyone at the sit-down said he was a stand-up guy, but he whacked a wise guy and then got popped for it. Then the squealer sang and ratted out his own skipper. He went into the program to avoid getting jammed up. The snitch."

There are goomba classics, too. The original *Oceans Eleven* is a goomba classic. *From Here to Eternity,* because of Frank. *Robin and the Seven Hoods,* same thing. Also, there's *Across 110th Street,* with Anthony Quinn. It's obscure, but every goomba knows it. Same with *The Killing of a Chinese Bookie,* with Ben Gazzara.

And there are movies that some goombas would never see. I don't personally agree, but some of them wouldn't see *Jungle Fever,* or any other Spike Lee movie, even though there's some Bensonhurst goomba scenes in *Do the Right Thing,* which stars a couple of great goomba actors, Danny Aiello and John Turturro. And goombas ain't going to see *Harry Potter,* or *Lord of the Rings.* We're not sitting still for *Titanic,* or any of that sentimental crap. No *Sound of Music.* "The hills are alive . . ." my ass. No *Singin' in the Rain.* No musicals at all. Nothing with singing. No Barbra Streisand, for God's sake. No singing, and no crying. No *Terms of Endearment.* No *Love Story.*

You wanna be amused? Watch *Little Rascals, Bowery Boys, Angels with Dirty Faces. Broadway Danny Rose.* It's not like we don't like to laugh. It's just that we don't want to see *Rush Hour 2.* You'd shoot yourself before you saw something like that.

And television is basically for sports. We goombas

don't watch sitcoms. We especially don't watch any-thing on Fox or the WB. Too ethnic. And the big net-work shows? Forget it. We don't watch *Friends*. We don't watch *The West Wing*. Too white, and not believ-able. We *might* watch a re-run of *Seinfeld*. We might watch some of the older shows, like *Columbo,* or *Baretta.* Those guys were cops, but they were cool, and they had Italian names. We watch *NYPD Blue,* for sure. We might watch *The King of Queens.* We watch Ray Romano, cause he's one of us. That's if we're watching TV at all. Which mostly we're not.

The goomba, see, he doesn't watch much (except sports). He *does* a lot of stuff, but he isn't much of a spectator. He'd rather do something than watch some-thing. He'd rather eat. Or cook. Or go out with the guys.

Goomba literature? The idea is almost a contra-diction. There aren't any classic goomba books. We don't read. I'm still trying to come up with a few titles. Maybe you'd read Mario Puzo, like . . . *The Godfather.* But why? You got the movie! Maybe it's *this* book. Maybe we'll get back to you.

As for sports and hobbies . . . Well, goombas don't have hobbies, and goombas don't play sports except maybe a game of bocci ball or pool, and those don't really count. Bocci is for old guys, and pool is just

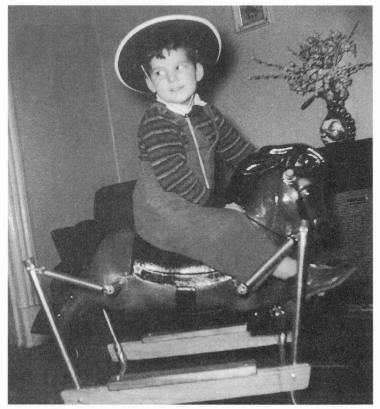

A goomba cowboy. Who said there were none?

something to do while you're drinking. Your average goomba doesn't play in the local softball league. That's for white guys, like hockey. He doesn't play pick-up basketball. That's for black guys, like dancing. You will never see a goomba on a tennis court. Or a golf course, unless he's on vacation in Florida or Arizona. A goomba will watch football, and baseball, because he's got money on it, but he will never play those sports. He'll watch the fights.

There are certain places you will never see a goomba, either. There are no goombas in Tennessee, or Minnesota, unless they're in the witness protection program. You will never see a goomba at the ballet. Or in the library. You will never see a goomba in a canoe. Or a hang glider. Never. You will never see a goomba hiking, unless he's on the lam and running through the woods.

There are some things we just don't do. You will never see a goomba on horseback. There is no such thing as a goomba cowboy. You will never see a goomba on skis. There are no goombas in the winter Olympics. There are also no goombas in the summer Olympics.

GOOMBA RULES AND REGULATIONS

BY NOW, you're probably saying to yourself: "Hey, this goomba thing sounds pretty good! How can I be a goomba? Could I be a goomba already without knowing it?" Here are some guidelines. If you can relate to

any of the following, you're probably well on your way
to being a goomba:

> You have more than two uncles with goomba names, like
> Vito, Vinnie, or Frankie.
>
> You have more than two uncles with women's names, like
> Sally, Angie, Julie, or Allie.
>
> You have more than one pinky ring.
>
> You first found out your father loved you by listening to a
> federal wire tap.
>
> Your speed dial only has numbers for your mother and your
> bookie—and you can place a bet with either one.
>
> Your father uses the Italian word for "eggplant" while
> watching a basketball game.

On the other hand, what if you're *not* a goomba? Even
if you're Italian, or Italian-American, if any of the
statements below apply, you're not a goomba.

> You don't own a copy of *The Godfather* on tape or DVD.
>
> You don't have any *Sinatra* music in your home.
>
> You don't have any *Sinatra* music in your car.
>
> You think Ellen De Generes is funny.
>
> You like the Grateful Dead.
>
> You drive a Japanese car.
>
> You attended the Million Man March.

GOOMBA NAMES

ANOTHER WAY TO identify the goomba easily is by his use of nicknames. Goombas *love* nicknames. Every self-respecting goomba has a nickname. However, there are certain names you can give a goomba, and certain names you can't.

Names that have hard sounds and end with vowels are best, like Rocco, Sammy, Nicky, and so on. All Italian names are automatically good: Angelo. Giorgio. Vito. Same way with the Italian names that have turned into American names; they can turn into good nicknames. Vincenzo turns into Vincent, which is very white-bread, but then it turns into Vinnie, which is an excellent goomba name. Arturo turns into Arthur, which is no good, but it turns into Artie, which is good. Tomaso turns into Thomas turns into Tommy. You get the idea.

Anthony is good. Michael is good. These all come from good Italian names, and they make good nicknames. "Hey, Tony! Hey, Mikie!" You can hear the goomba in that.

Stuck-up sounding British names, on the other hand, are no good. You can't call a goomba something like Roger or Reginald with a straight face. I mean, listen to it: "Hey, Reg! Hey, Rog!" It won't work.

And please, even though you might think it's cute, don't name your goomba kids any of those private school, suburban, SUV names. You ruin a kid's chances of ever being a goomba if you call him Courtney, or Cameron, or Justin, or Jason, or Shawn. Imagine what that sounds like in a goomba context.

"Who's coming Friday night?"

"Everybody! We got Sal and Angie and Vito, and Vinnie, and Mikie, and Rocco. Oh yeah, and Harper and Madison are coming, too."

GOOMBAS VERSUS GANGSTERS

I'VE BEEN AROUND wise guys all my life. There were guys I grew up with that went that way. I see 'em around, and we talk, and it's very nice and friendly. I don't ask what they do. They don't tell me what they do. Hey, there's no statute of limitations on murder! Most wise guys don't talk shop.

That doesn't stop them from letting me know what they think about *my* job, though. Occasionally one of these guys will tell me he doesn't like something about *The Sopranos*. Sometimes, it's pretty tough. My friend Joey Pants—Joe Pantoliano, he's on the show—was on a talk show and he said *The Sopranos* doesn't glorify wise

Me and Mister Pants.

guys, as some critics had complained. He said *The Sopranos* showed wise guys the way they really *are*—not the clichés, but the truth. Not long after that, he got a message from a very big, very tough guy: Shut up with that stuff, or someone will make you shut up.

I haven't had anything like that, but a guy did complain to me recently about one scene. It was a scene where a guy got clipped. Someone snuck up on him, in the street, and killed him from behind or something. And this wise guy I met said, "Hey! Anybody who knows anything knows you don't kill a guy that way! Anybody knows that!" Well, maybe a wise guy knows that.

It's funny, because a lot of people think we *are* glorifying the mob, or apologizing for the mob. That's ridiculous. Look at the show. These are not nice people.

These are bad guys. They don't just hurt each other, either. They hurt innocent people. They do very bad things to innocent people. They rob and they steal, and they extort money from people, and shake people down. These are despicable guys, some of them. And we show that, every week.

I think *The Sopranos* is a story that needs to be told. It's a real slice of Italian-American life. It doesn't mean all Italian-Americans are like this, or even that a lot of them are like this. But let's not kid ourselves: This stuff is *real*. It's happening. And it's important that someone show that.

But don't confuse gangsters with goombas. Goomba is different. Here's a handy rule: Gangsters, bad. Goombas, good. Simple!

GOOMBA LINGO

BACK TO the language lessons. If you're going to act like a goomba, you gotta talk like a goomba. What you say is just as important as what you don't say. Here are some useful abbreviations:

Feds—The federal government, specifically the Federal
Bureau of Investigation

IRS—Your worst nightmare, since hiding money is the key to hiding illegal activity.

IOU—A handy abbreviation that means, "I am broke right now, but if you give me money, I might pay you back, someday."

LCN—La Cosa Nostra, or the Maria

On the other hand, there are some abbreviations, popular in American culture, that are never spoken by goombas. You will never hear a goomba use these expressions—or the activities they stand for:

MTV

VH-1

UPS

RSVP

WD-40

WWJD

HOW TO BE A GOOMBA—*NOT*

JUST AS there are expressions you'd never use and places you'd never be, there are some things that a real goomba would never do. The following story is a very good illustration. This is about a guy who probably thinks he's a sort of goomba. The story shows that he is almost the opposite.

This guy I know, he's a big cheese in the entertainment industry. And he's a big, big gambler. He gambles on everything—the fights, the ponies, the ball games, everything. Like most gamblers, he loses. And because he's a big gambler, he loses big.

At one point, he was into a couple of loan sharks for about $50,000. These were bad guys, these loan sharks. They were getting...restless. They wanted their money! And they let him know, quietly at first, and then not so quietly, that this situation was starting to be not so healthy. When that didn't work, they told the guy, "You got a week, and then we're coming with the kneecap machine."

The guy freaks out. He knows these guys, and he knows they're serious. And he's got no way to get the money. He's borrowed everything he can borrow, from everyone he knows, to pay for gambling debts in the past. Everyone has told him no.

So he comes up with a plan.

He knows these guys who aren't gangsters but who have *played* gangsters in the movies. They're actors. They're goomba actors, from the neighborhood, but they're still actors. He hires them to pretend to be wise guys—hit men, in fact, for the mob loan sharks. He promises to pay them a grand each.

And he sends them to his mother's house.

See, he knows his mother has some money in the bank. He knows she won't give him any more to settle gambling debts, because he has asked and asked and asked. But he thinks she might give it up if the right pressure was applied, by the right guys.

So he sends them to her house. They bust in, and they tell the old lady, "We got your son. He owes us $50,000. If we don't have the money by the end of the day, we'll kill him."

Naturally the old lady goes to the bank and gets the money.

To this day, she has no idea the guys that were going to kill her son were just goomba actors. She thinks she saved his life. Which, in fact, she did—just not the way she thinks. If the guy hadn't hired the goomba actors, and gotten the money, the *real* bad guys might have come after him with something heavy.

Now, here's the moral of this story: The big cheese who started all this stuff is not Italian. He is not a goomba. That is obvious to any real goomba because a real goomba would never, never, never—in a thousand years, never—do something like this to his mother. A real goomba would wait for the hard guys to show up and he'd sit there patiently watching while they shot his kneecaps off before he'd let any loan shark near his poor old mother. He would kneecap *himself* before he'd let anyone touch his mother. There's a lot of bad things a goomba might do, and there's bad things that a goomba gambler in trouble will definitely do. But nothing like this. It's beneath contempt, from the goomba point of view.

So, act like a goomba if you want. Be a tough guy, and get into trouble, and get out of trouble—just like the goombas in the movies. But remember: Never, ever jeopardize your family. That's one of the goomba golden rules.

GOOMBA CHUTZPAH

THERE IS ONE final characteristic that sets the goomba apart from his unfortunate non-goomba brothers, but I don't know what you call it. The Mexicans—and my wife is Mexican, so I know—call it "*cojones.*" The Jews—and my mother is Jewish, so I know—call it "*chutzpah.*" I've heard people talk about "nerve," and about "gall," and about "moxie." What it means is . . . *balls.* Stones. Eggs. And the goomba has got a lot of that. The goomba is a guy with a lot of *cojones*. We might say about a guy like that, "He should carry his balls in a wheelbarrow," or, "He's sure got cogliones."

One of my pals is Joe Gannascoli. He's an actor on *The Sopranos,* a great guy, and a great goomba. What nerve! The guy's got balls like cantaloupes! Here's what I'm talking about.

Joe wanted to be a chef. He worked in some of the best restaurants in New York, as a sort of third-level cook. He'd prep and chop and wash and whatnot, but he wanted to be a real chef. He left New York and went down to New Orleans, where a friend of his was living. He needed a job. So he walked right into Antoine's—maybe the oldest and most famous restaurant in the French Quarter—and said he needed a job. The chef asked him what he did in New York. Joe said, "I did everything. I'm a friggin chef!" So the guy hired him and put him on the line.

The first night on the job, they put Joe on the fish station. He's mostly doing oysters. They've got, like, fifteen or twenty oyster dishes on the menu and they do something like seven hundred dinners a night. So from the minute he starts, Joe's shucking oysters and hurling them into sauces and onto plates. And he's got no idea what he's doing. Oysters Rockefeller? Oysters Antoine? He don't know one from the other. And almost right away the plates start coming back. This is the wrong sauce. That is the wrong order. They fire him on the spot.

Within a week, he's done it again—talked himself into another job in another high-class New Orleans joint. This one is Commander's Palace, which is the place where Paul Prudhomme and Emeril Lagasse, the

great chefs of modern New Orleans, got their start. What nerve! Another guy would've slunk out of town, or started driving a cab. Not Joe. Today he runs his own restaurant in Brooklyn, called Soup as Art.

And that nerve of his got him his start in show business, too. He had done a little theater work in New York, and he went out to LA. But he couldn't get anything going. Same old story: You need an agent to get work, but until you've got work the agents don't want to talk to you. So here's what he did. He learned about a guy who got the breakdowns—the list of auditions coming up—sent to his home at six o'clock every morning. Joe staked out his house. As soon as the casting call was delivered, he'd steal 'em, and run over to a photocopy place, and copy 'em, and return 'em, before the guy knew they were missing. Then he'd call the casting agents and pretend to be his own talent agent. He'd say his name was James Hoving, and he represented Joe Gannascoli, and he wanted to make sure this casting agent saw his client for such-and-such a part. He'd send his own head shot over, and make the follow-up call to the casting people to see how he did on the audition.

He started getting work. And he was so successful getting himself work, as James Hoving, that James Hoving started making calls on behalf of Joe's other actor friends. He started getting *them* work, too. One time he called a casting agent who was looking for a guy to play Bobby Kennedy. He told them his client was a terrific actor. The agent asked could he really play Bobby Kennedy? James Hoving said, "Are you kidding? I saw him in a one-man show, off-Broadway, where he played *all three* Kennedys. It was called, uh, *Bobby, Teddy and Me.*" There never was any such show, of course, but his client got the audition.

That's real goomba stuff. As Joe says, "If you got balls, and you got persistence, you can do anything in the world."

This is getting clearer and clearer. If you're still confused, or you're having a goomba identity crisis, use the handy checklist below.

STALKING THE WILD GOOMBA

BY NOW, you know exactly what the goomba looks like, dresses like, acts like, and sounds like. You know what he eats, and what he listens to, and what he watches on TV. But where do you find him? Stalking the goomba in his natural habitat isn't all that difficult. You go to Brooklyn. You go to Bensonhurst. You walk up Bath

YOU MIGHT BE A GOOMBA IF ... CONTINUED

Your godfather *is* a godfather.

Your wife and your girlfriend are cousins.

You use the term "fat bastard" to show affection.

Your mother taught you how to shave.

Every guy at your wedding was called Tony.

You think getting a slice is a romantic dinner.

You have an everyday sweat suit and a going-out sweat suit.

Avenue. You're surrounded! But what if you're somewhere else, and you think you see goombas? How can you be sure?

It's easier than you think. There are some places you will *never* see a real goomba:

> You will never find a goomba at a Marriage Encounters Weekend.
>
> You will never find a goomba at a rodeo.
>
> You will never find a goomba getting a pedicure.
>
> You will never find a goomba in a thong.
>
> You will never find a goomba in a rocket ship—we ain't going into space.
>
> You will never find a goomba in a backpack.
>
> You will never find a goomba at a Britney Spears concert.
>
> You will never find a goomba at a Subway or Quizno's.
>
> You will never find a goomba in a Kia.

Chapter 2

GOOMBA LIFE

No self-respecting goomba

likes being out of work.

Your average goomba may

be a lazy guy . . . but

he ain't no bum.

By now you have a pretty good idea what I'm talking about when I say goomba, but maybe you're asking yourself: How does a guy get to be a goomba? Is a goomba born or made? (Not, mind you, *made* with a capital M.) The answer is: it's a little of both. Take me for example.

My family life was pretty nutty. My father is Italian, born in the United States, but Italian-American. My mother is Jewish, but she grew up in an Italian neighborhood, surrounded by Italians. She was raised by people who spoke Italian and cursed Italian and cooked Italian. She wound up half-Italian, or more than half.

My whole life was mixed up that way. The neighborhood where I grew up was all Italian. But when I went to high school, it was half Italian and half Jewish. I played basketball in college, and later I tried out for a basketball team from Tel Aviv. And when I moved out to Las Vegas, one of my first jobs was making sandwiches in a Jewish deli. And my next job was delivering pizzas for these two guys from Brooklyn.

Growing up was pretty crazy. Like most goomba families, ours was a *loud* family. Everyone yelled. No one spoke. You had to scream if you wanted to be heard, because everyone else was screaming. Who started the screaming, I don't know, but once it was on, there was no stopping it. Everyone yelled at everyone all the time, no matter what else was going on.

And the food was terrific, especially at my grandmother's house. My grandmother used to serve a big Sunday dinner. The whole family would come—maybe fifteen to twenty people. It was a typical goomba day. The men would watch the ball game. The women would cook and gossip.

Sunday night would start with pasta, always. Then there'd be roast beef or chicken or maybe veal. My grandmother would serve at one o'clock in the afternoon. The men would all drink red wine, or maybe a beer if it was a hot day. And everyone would yell, all through the meal. Some people would yell in English, and some would yell in Italian, and some would yell in

A typical Sunday at Gramma's.

half-English, half-Italian. That's goomba—goombataliano. It would go like this:

> "Five bucks, for a prosciutto di Parma."
> "Five bucks? *Che pazzo.*"
> "Cheap bastid. Pass the *vitello.*"

We'd eat, and we'd argue, and then we'd rest. The men would take a nap in front of the television. The women would clean up. Then at five o'clock the yelling and the eating would start all over again.

~ ~ ~

GOOMBA KIDS AIN'T any different from other kids, but they grow up in a different world. There's a lot of affection, physical and otherwise. Lots of hugging. Lots of, "C'mere and kiss your Uncle Cosmo, you little brat." There's a lot of violence, too, mental and otherwise. Plus, it's a city childhood. Your goomba family doesn't grow up in the suburbs. There's none of that Sunday school, car pool, Boy Scout troop, hula-hoop, choir practice, T-ball team stuff. No one's playing flag football. No one's having bake sales. No one belongs to the PTA. The kids don't go to cotillion or karate class. The kids are in the street, playing stickball. Or they're in the schoolyard, playing softball. No one's sitting outside, tending the barbecue, holding a gin and tonic and discussing the stock market. No one's down at the stable, grooming Thundercloud the thoroughbred. No one's down in the pasture throwing the Frisbee for Fido the dog.

In fact, hardly anyone has animals. That's one of the big differences between goomba households and, say, WASP households. We don't keep pets.

There are exceptions. For a while we had this horrible dog. It was my mother's dog. She called it Martini. But something was wrong with this dog. It bit people. It bit *everybody*. In some families, this would have been a good reason to get rid of the dog. Not my family. My mother did the only other intelligent thing she could think of—she had the dog's teeth removed. Every last tooth. Now the dog looked like my grandmother—it was toothless and it drooled all the time. But unfortunately, the dog didn't change his behavior. Now, instead of biting you, it's *gumming* you to death. I hated that dog.

The only other pet I ever had was a rabbit. It was this big gorgeous rabbit that we named Sniffy. I was about seven years old. I loved that rabbit more than anything, but it started getting big. Finally the landlord told us we had to get rid of it. I was crushed. My mother told me it would be okay, that she was going to give Sniffy to this lady named Mrs. Parmesi, from the neighborhood. She told us Mrs. Parmesi had some family with a farm, upstate. Sniffy would live on this farm, happily ever after.

Six months later I met Mrs. Parmesi on the street. I said, "How's Sniffy?" She says, "What are you talking about?" I said, "How's Sniffy. The rabbit? How's the rabbit we gave you?" And she said, "It was delicious! We made a beautiful Easter dinner with it."

You can imagine I was pretty upset. To this day, I couldn't eat rabbit if it was that or starving to death. Mrs. Parmesi ruined it for me, for life.

I still feel weird about rabbits. Years later, I was the entertainment director for the Riviera Hotel in Las Vegas. We were planning an Easter show. So, naturally enough, I booked a "Mr. and Mrs. Bunny" act to come in and perform. I never met them. I booked them through some agency. So they showed up, costumes on, wearing these big rabbit heads and rabbit costumes, head to toe. And they were terrific. People who come to Las Vegas love that sort of stuff.

But there was some kind of problem with the air conditioning. Halfway through the show, Mr. Bunny comes backstage. He's all overheated. He's dying. He has to take his head off, so he can cool down. So he takes off the rabbit head, and he's Elvis! The guy's an Elvis impersonator! I say, "Wait a minute! I booked Mr. Bunny. You're Elvis!" He says, "Yeah, I'm Elvis. I only do Mr. Bunny when it's slow. Right now, it's real slow. And sometimes I'm Roy Orbison." And he put his rabbit head back on and went back out and finished his bit.

You'd think I'd have a Playboy bunny story to tell, too. But I don't. Only Sniffy and Elvis.

~ ~ ~

A LOT OF my childhood memories are centered around food. I was a big kid, a growing boy, and I was hungry a lot of the time. I was very active, very physical, and I loved to eat. Maybe that explains it.

There was a guy in my neighborhood when I was growing up. He sold hot dogs and pretzels out of the back of his station wagon. He'd drive around the neighborhood, selling hot dogs and pretzels. Delicious! His name was Fat Farouk. I don't know where the "Farouk" part came from. But I know where they got the "Fat" part. The guy was huge. He'd park the station wagon, and when he got out, the car moved *up*, like, three feet. He was enormous. He weighed something like four hundred pounds. No, I'm exaggerating. He weighed *at least* six hundred pounds.

All the kids used to make fun of him. He didn't seem to notice. And the kids all bought pretzels and hot dogs and sodas from him. They'd say, "Yo, Fat Farouk! How'd you get so fat? Gimme a hot dog!" He'd growl and give 'em the hot dog.

One day he comes down the street and parks the car and gets out. The car goes up three feet. Then he goes around and lowers the tailgate, and sits on the tailgate. The car goes down three feet. I'm going over there to buy a hot dog. When I get there, Fat Farouk is sitting on the tailgate with no shoes or socks on. He says to me, "Howya doon, kid? You want an orange drink?" I say, "Whatta I gotta do?" He says, "You gotta put my sock on, kid."

He sticks this big fat foot at me. He's so fat, he can't bend over to put on a sock. So I put it on for him, and he gives me an orange drink. Then he says, "You want a pretzel?" I say, "Whatta I gotta do?" He says, "You gotta put my other sock on." Then he gave me a pretzel.

Here's the weird part. Fat as he was, and as much food as he dragged around with him, Fat Farouk never ate a pretzel or a hot dog. He didn't touch the merchandise. How come? Who knows? Maybe one of the neighborhood tough guys owned Farouk's business, and the inventory. Maybe he couldn't eat his own cooking. Maybe he was afraid that if he started eating he wouldn't quit until the pretzels and the hot dogs and the station wagon were all gone. I don't know. I never asked. I don't know what became of Fat Farouk.

A GOOMBA TEENAGER: THE HOODLUM YEARS

MAYBE IT was hanging around Fat Farouk so much as a kid that made me think there was some kind of connection between food and crime. Or maybe it was just because I was always hungry. But there was a time,

Broke again in Florida. Spring break 1978.

when I was a teenager, when I turned into a criminal. Not a thief, exactly—because that's a real profession—but a sort of hoodlum, a part-time thief. And all I ever stole was food.

Here's the deal. Me and a bunch of friends, one summer, started doing the old dine-and-ditch thing. We were broke, all the guys in the neighborhood, and we were always hungry, and we were hangin' out on the corner and we were seventeen or eighteen years old. There was, like, twenty of us. So we started stealing.

At first, it was sort of a gag. We'd go into a pizza joint, two or three of us, and order a pizza, and when it hit the counter we'd grab the pizza and hit the door. Or we'd hit a diner for food to go. We'd order enough for five or six guys. (We'd actually take orders from the guys on the corner. Whatta you want? Whatta you want? One guy wants this, another guy wants that. We'd write it all down, like we were going to the supermarket or something.) Two guys would go into the diner and place the order for food to go. One guy would wait outside in the getaway car.

Soon as the food hit the counter, boom! We're out the door! And into the car and away we go.

We'd hit Chinese restaurants. We'd hit diners. We'd steal bagels and pizzas. Whatever! Our only rule was we never, ever hit a wiseguy place, or an Italian place. That could only bring trouble.

As time went on, we made up all kinds of clever schemes to make it safer, and to order even more food.

For example, we'd call a Chinese place and order some food to be delivered to, say, 105 16th Avenue. Then we'd call the Chinese place again and order some more food for a different apartment, on the same block, like at 110 16th Street. They'd think they were having a big night in Bensonhurst—two orders, at the same time, on the same block!

We'd wait for the guy to drive up. He'd go inside to make the first delivery—to this phony address, who knows who lives there?—and we'd go for his car. Because we know there's food in there, for the second order.

The goomba, he ain't stupid!

But we started having trouble. One time, we went into this Subway sandwich joint and ordered sandwiches for, like, twenty people. Then the guy I'm with recognizes the guy behind the counter. They went to junior high school together. Now the guy behind the counter recognizes him, too. It's too late to do anything about the sandwiches. We'd ordered them. And we don't have enough to pay for them, even if we want to. So my friend, he decides to come clean with his old junior high school buddy. But he wants the sandwiches. So he takes him aside and explains the whole thing: We're hungry, and we're broke, and we're the guys from your neighborhood, and your boss is a creep, and he'll never know. The guy buys it! We got out with the sandwiches.

Another night, though, it didn't go that good. It's three o'clock in the morning. We're in a Greek diner. There's four or five of us. We've eaten a big meal. We're getting ready to dine-and-ditch. And then these cops come in. And they sit down to have dinner. We don't have a dollar between us to pay for the meal. So we decide we gotta run. So we get ready and bang! Out the door, up the street, across a vacant lot! But there's two guys chasing us. So we split up. Everybody goes in a different direction. And for some reason the two guys *both* stick with me! I run like crazy and then hide under a bush. But they find me. I know they're gonna take me back to the diner and turn me over to the cops. And first they're getting ready to rough me up. This is bad.

So I do a little reverse goomba psychology. I say to these two guys, "You don't know who my uncle is. You hit me and it's gonna be very, very bad for you."

This is the kind of neighborhood it is: The guys stop. They *gotta* stop. They gotta think, "Wait. Who is this kid? Who's his uncle?"

So they decide to take me back to the diner. They don't say anything to the cops, because guys like that don't talk to cops. Instead, they make me call some-one's father to come down and give up the money. It's five in the morning! But it's better than taking a beatin' or going to jail, so I make the call.

That was pretty much the end of it. We stopped the dine-and-ditch operation after that. It was fun, but it wasn't worth it. Easier to get a job and just pay for the stuff.

GOOMBAS ON THE JOB

YOU'LL HEAR a lot of joking about how lazy the goomba is. He don't lift nothing heavier than a fork—stuff like that. But most of the goombas I know are hard-working guys. They have to be. Your average goomba is just another middle-class working stiff. He's got bills to pay, same as everybody else. He might like to spend the days sipping espresso and the nights chatting with pole dancers—and who the hell wouldn't—but he can't support himself and his family that way. And most goombas I know, they think supporting their family is job number one. They think having a job, and doing a good job, and getting paid well for it, is part of being a man.

They got it the same way I did—from being a kid. I'm not saying every goomba grew up the same way I did, but this is what happened to me.

My father was a bookmaker for the mob. He had an office in Coney Island, where he did his business—taking bets on the horses or the ball games, collecting bets, moving the line—and there were always neighborhood guys in and out of our apartment in Brooklyn. They all had classic goomba names. There was Joe Bananas, and a guy called Lefty, and a guy called Bubbie. There was

Bennie Eggs and Sally Bim. Patty Cabbage. Petie Boxcars. Real Bensonhurst characters. There was a social club on the corner where they all played cards and hung out all day. And there were certain nights when they'd all go out together. They'd get very dressed up, sharp suits and neckties, and go out drinking.

My father had these outfits. He'd go out wearing green shoes, green pants, a green shirt and tie, and a green jacket—and green socks. Where the hell do you find an outfit like that? I still don't know, but he had tons of 'em, in several different colors. Blue jacket, blue shoes, blue shirt and tie, blue socks. All coordinated. He was a very sharp dresser. He was a little guy, like 5'8" and 140 pounds—not big, like me—but a very sharp dresser.

My uncle and dad. Sharp guys.

Life was good in those days for the growing goomba family. My father worked steady

and he always had money. He
always had big wads of money.
And we always had stuff—
swag. There were always new
suits and leather jackets. My
mother always had a fur. We
had a movie projector. He was
always coming through the
door with these boxes of
things we didn't have, and
didn't even know we wanted.
New things, that had some-
how mysteriously appeared in
his hands. We didn't ask where
they came from. We knew we

My mom, before things went bad.

weren't supposed to ask questions like that.

My father did a little business on the side with some
of that stuff. He always had illegal cigarettes for sale. Or
liquor. Or perfume. The stuff would just appear in the
house. He'd bring in a case of liquor, and it would sit in
the hallway for a couple of days, and then it would be
gone. Racks of clothing would come and go. He was
getting the stuff from one place, illegally, and selling it
another place, illegally. I don't know how much his boss
knew about what he was doing on the side. Again, this
wasn't a question anyone was going to ask.

Then, one day, the cops came in and raided our house. It was the Friday before Easter. My father wasn't home. The cops came in and started busting up the place. They were looking for papers from my father's bookmaking operations. And they found what they were looking for—enough evidence to make an arrest.

But since my father wasn't there, they arrested my mother. She spent Easter in jail.

That was pretty scary, for a kid. Me, my three sisters, and brother had to spend Easter with my grandmother.

After he started getting arrested, things started going bad for our family. He had thirty-two arrests and numerous convictions. He wound up doing time at Riker's Island—two stints there, and some time someplace else. For bookmaking. For the mob.

From then on, we were always on welfare. Food stamps. We had to hock all the swag. The phone was turned off. The electricity was turned off. My father got out of jail, and he came home, but didn't want to make book anymore. Too bad; it turned out it was the only thing he was good at. He couldn't make it doing anything else. He couldn't hold down a straight job and provide for his family. It's weird to say it, but he should've stayed with the mob. That's what he was good at. That's all he knew.

Because my father couldn't support his family, I

started working when I was pretty young. And I had all kinds of jobs growing up. For a while I worked at Colonial Mansion. This was a place in Bensonhurst, right on Bath Avenue, that did all the catering jobs. We catered every event imaginable. If something important was happening, we catered it. An engagement party, an anniversary party, a wedding, a funeral, whatever—this was where you went to get it catered. I had a job as a dishwasher for a while, and then I got promoted to porter. That meant instead of washing dishes I was vacuuming floors. Big step up.

Every day, the owner would come to the place. Everyone would stop, and line up, and wait. It was like the Pope was coming through. We'd all stand and wait. If he liked you, he'd give you a big tip. I was making three dollars an hour, and he'd tip me sometimes five bucks. Which at that time, to me, was a lot of money.

I worked hard, but I didn't necessarily *enjoy* working hard. I was just a young goomba, and I was kind of lazy. I worked, always, but I wasn't one of those guys who loved going to work. Sometimes I worked harder at looking like I was working than at actually working.

Here's an example. I had a job in my early twenties, as a chimney sweep. I was on commission. I was paid a certain amount of money for every chimney I cleaned. They'd give me the address, and I'd go out with my brushes and my vacuums. It was fifty-four bucks for the cleaning, I think, and I got ten dollars for each one.

Half the time, though, the fireplace didn't need cleaning at all. The chimney was clear. So I'd just wave the brushes around on the roof and then clean the fireplace out and that was that. I'd light a piece of paper and wave it around in the fireplace, to show the chimney was clear, for the grand finale.

A lot of the time, the people wouldn't even be at home. The superintendent would let me in. And so I'd take it easy. I was just a young goomba, and I had lots of things on my mind. So, I'd open the refrigerator, crack open a beer, and put on some music. Maybe I'd have a nap. Watch a little TV. Make a sandwich. Read a magazine. I did everything except steal. I didn't steal, 'cause that's hard work, too. You gotta find the stuff, and then get the stuff out of the apartment, and then fence the stuff, and then not get caught, and if you get caught you have to go to jail . . . Hard work! It was easier to take the ten dollars and have a beer and a sandwich.

Your goomba is a lazy man, basically. He takes care of business, but he'll take it easy if he can.

Some guys do that by hooking up with the mob. A lot of guys I grew up with turned into wise guys. I'm not even sure how it happened. But it happened.

These were guys I knew from when I was a little kid.

Goombas in Vegas, 1981.

They were guys I played baseball with, and stickball. In the winter, we played football. We were on the church team, St. Francis Cabrini. These were guys I went to elementary school with, and junior high school, and high school. I wouldn't say they were any different, in any way, from any of the other guys. They weren't tougher, or more crooked, or smarter, or stupider, or anything. They were just guys—young goombas, like me and the other guys.

But somewhere in there, usually somewhere in high school, you'd start to notice which way guys were

- 57 -

heading. Some guys were doing good in high school, and they were talking about college, or the service. Other guys . . . they started hanging out with guys we didn't know. They start dressing a little better. They started driving newer cars. They started driving cars in the first place. I'm riding the bus to school, and here's a guy driving a Camaro. I'm scraping pennies together to get a bite at McDonald's, and these guys are talking about eating in fancy restaurants. You notice stuff like that.

No self-respecting goomba likes being out of work, though. Your average goomba may be a lazy guy who's happy to let his wife do the dishes, but he ain't no bum. He'll do what it takes to pay the bills. For me, I worked on a soft drink delivery truck, sold fruit and fish at a shop in Little Italy, delivered pizzas, was a security guard at concerts, was a security guard at a disco roller-rink (that shows you exactly how old I am), and worked for the U.S. Postal Service, as a mail-sorter. I was a baseball umpire for hire. I was a basketball referee. I shucked clams. I washed dishes. I was a bouncer.

These are all fine jobs for the young goomba. Here are some other employment opportunities you might want to consider if you're thinking of becoming a goomba yourself.

Bookie

Union official

Teamster driver

Sanitation worker

Bar/nightclub owner

Candy store owner

Actor

I know one goomba dentist and one goomba doctor. But there aren't too many of those. I know one goomba barber. That's a borderline goomba occupation.

There are some occupations, on the other hand, that a goomba should avoid. Like, there is never going to be a goomba astronaut—'cause your goomba is too smart for that. Let another guy go to the moon. Me, I'm staying right here.

Here are some jobs a goomba will never do:

Manicurist	Dance instructor
Museum curator	Brain surgeon
Librarian	Make-up artist

Rodeo clown	Police informer
Interior decorator	Dancer in *Cats*
Fashion designer	

It starts like this. One of the guys from the neighborhood will get a job, sweeping up or washing dishes, in one of the social clubs where the wise guys hang out. Maybe they let him work the espresso machine or make the sandwiches. Maybe he starts running errands and driving guys around. That's where the transformation starts. He's just a guy from the neighborhood, and he's no different from the other guys in the neighborhood, but now he's working for guys that you don't really know. And he's got money. And he's sort of connected.

Pretty soon, from there, he's getting bigger errands to do. He's starting to sell a little dope, maybe. Or he's bookmaking. Or he's collecting money for the bookmaker. Maybe he's stealing stuff. It's like having an internship. You're learning the ropes.

Later on in life, if you know what to look for, you can always separate the real wise guys from the wannabe wise guys. The frauds are flashing a lot of money, so that everybody sees, and they're always going around with loud broads with big tits, and they're always saying stuff like, "Drinks on the house," or "Hey paisan', how ya doin'?" They got huge pinky rings and flashy suits and they want everybody in the joint to know who they are. They might even ask you, "You know who I am, right? You know who I work for, right?" They really shove it in your face.

The real wise guys? Used to be, you'd never notice them. They'd sit in the back, minding their own business, keeping their mouths shut and their eyes open. Until some of the modern guys started showing up on TV more often than re-runs of *The Honeymooners*, the real wise guys were almost invisible. Now they're like celebrities. That changed everything. So it's hard to know who's what.

In my neighborhood, for a while, stealing spare tires was a big business for the kids: This was back when most cars had a real tire for the spare—not the little donuts they put in there nowadays. Guys would go out of the neighborhood—you definitely didn't want to steal a tire from a wise guy on your block—and cruise around until they found a nice car. They'd drill a hole in the trunk, pop the lock out with a screwdriver, and steal the spare. Steal four, and you've got a whole set of new tires, with wheels. This was a big business—hundreds of thousands of dollars over the years.

For some guys it was a way to make a little money on the side. For other guys, it was a kind of apprenticeship for a life of crime. Most guys, they just went on with their lives. Not all of them.

Some goombas make a life out of crime. Some of them turn into big-time gangsters.

GOOMBAS AND GANGSTERS IN VEGAS

A PLACE WHERE the line between goombas and gangsters gets pretty fuzzy is Vegas. There's all kinds of Italians in Las Vegas. Always have been. But it's like an Italian smorgasbord. There's New York Italians, Chicago Italians, Cleveland Italians, Buffalo Italians, Detroit Italians.

They used to be organized by casino. Each group was affiliated with the casino they were behind. The Dunes was a New York hotel. The Aladdin was Detroit. The Stardust was Chicago. The Desert Inn was Cleveland.

In the old days, each of these groups had its own favorite restaurants. There were places that, everyone knew, served Chicago Italian, or Brooklyn Italian. The Brooklyn guys didn't eat at the Chicago joints, and vice versa.

But here's the funny thing. Back home, you would never trust a guy from Cincinnati, or Rhode Island, or

Boston. Or even Brooklyn. The neighborhood thing, that's very territorial. You meet a guy from Canarsie, or Greenpoint, even, and you're from Bensonhurst? There might be trouble.

But in Las Vegas, *everybody's* from the neighborhood. A guy from Brooklyn, a guy from Connecticut, it's all the same thing. A goomba is a goomba, and everybody's friends. And lots of them were crooked.

And no matter what anyone else tells you, a lot of the goombas that settled the desert were wise guys. I knew a lot of them, even though I got there after the great goomba heyday in Las Vegas. I knew Anthony Spilotro, because he was in Jubilation—the nightclub owned by Paul Anka—all the time. Same with Lefty Rosenthal. They were the guys played by Robert De Niro and Joe Pesci in *Casino*.

I was the bouncer at Jubilation. For a goomba kid from Bensonhurst, it was heaven. I was twenty-two years old, with ten cents in my pocket. I was nobody, from nowhere, but I'd put on a tuxedo and go to work, and suddenly I'm dating showgirls! And there were wise guys all over the place.

Herbie Blitstein was a great guy who was around all the time in those days. He was known as Fat Herbie. He was Spilotro's right-hand man. He trusted me with helping set up his son's wedding. We held it at the club.

One of my biggest jobs was to double-check the guests at the door, to make sure no FBI got into the wedding. Paul Anka sang at the reception. That's how important a guy like Fat Herbie Blitstein was.

Unfortunately, after the Spilotro period, Herbie made friends with the wrong guys. He ran a little credit card business, but he got caught and went to jail. When he got out, he still had a loan shark business. But some of his friends decided they wanted the business for themselves. So Herbie got killed. He's out in the desert somewhere. There's lots of guys out in the desert somewhere.

One of the big differences is that the casinos in those days were all run by goomba-type guys who were gamblers at heart. They made all their money from gambling. They understood gamblers, and gambling, and everything they did was for the gamblers. Shows didn't cost much. Dinner didn't cost much. The rooms were practically free. And no one got paid too much because it was all tips and cash.

This has completely changed the working situation for goombas with jobs in Las Vegas.

These days Vegas is run by corporations and every department has to make money. Every area has its own bottom line. Even the coffee shop has to turn a profit.

It's about families and predictable revenue. It's lost all the color and the romance.

I remember my friend Charles Najjar telling me about this time when he was working at the Hilton. One of the pit bosses was friggin out because a high-roller was hitting it big. He kept calling his manager and telling him, "We got a problem. The guy's really beating us." Finally, the guy had made $100,000, and he wasn't slowing down. This was in the 1960s, when that was a ton of money. So he calls the manager and says, "We gotta get rid of this guy."

The manager came over and said, "You eat yet?" The guys says, "You're not listening! This guy's killing us!" And the manager says, "Come on. Let's go eat." Over dinner, he says, "Leave the guy alone. Let him play. Time is on our side." The guy says, "But he's taken us for $100,000 already." The manager just smiles. He says, "I promise you, he will lose it all, in the end—if we let him keep playing. Time is on our side."

The guy ended up $40,000 down. He lost the $100,000, plus $40,000 more of his own money. Nobody had to trick him. Nobody did anything illegal. They didn't have to. Time is on the side of the house.

Another guy that knew the gambling game was Sid Wyman. He was a bookmaker from St. Louis who

wound up running the Dunes Hotel. He really understood gamblers. If a high-roller came in, he recognized
him. He'd see a guy who was a $5,000 player, and he'd
grab him before he even put down a bet. He'd say, "How
nice to see you again! How are you doing? Have you
eaten?" He'd take the guy to the Sultan's Table, which
was the fancy restaurant, and introduce him to the
maitre d'. The guy would have a great meal, on the
house, serenaded by violins, with wine and everything,
because Sid knew he'd leave the restaurant a $10,000
player.

And it wasn't just the high-rollers. My friend Vinnie
Montalto, who knew the Dunes well in those days, says
Sid used to get $500 to $1,000 in cash out of the cage
every morning, in small denominations. He'd walk
through the sports book. He'd see rounders that he was
friendly with—rounders are guys that hang around,
placing bets, looking for games, whatever—who were
down on their luck. He'd peel off a twenty or a fifty,
and he'd say, "How's it going? How're you playing?
Here's $20. Make a bet. Maybe it'll change your luck."

Can you imagine a casino operator doing that
today? Wandering around his own casino, handing out
twenty-dollar bills to guys who are not feeling lucky?
Impossible.

On the other hand, Vinnie remembers a guy who

used to come in and yell at the dealers when his luck was bad. He was a wise guy who had a lot of money. He'd come in and bet big. When he lost, he'd scream at the pit boss, "You're all against me, you bastards." So Sid took him aside. He said, "You come into my joint to be a sucker. So, be a sucker. But be a quiet sucker, or get out." That shut him up.

Can you imagine a hotel owner doing that now? No way.

In those days, if you were a gambler, everyone knew you. You'd check in to the hotel, and all the guys working the floor would already know you were there. They'd know what games you liked to play, how you liked to bet, what you liked to do when you weren't gambling. They were there to make you comfortable and keep you playing. And they all knew who was good for it, and who wasn't, and for how much.

These days, the gamblers come in and register and get "rated." If you gamble with a certain kind of chip, for a certain amount of time, you get rated at a certain level. The best is "RFB"—that means you're rated for "room, food, and beverage." Everything is free. If you don't gamble with big money, for several hours a day, you lose your RFB rating. And they sit you down and tell you all this, like it's a contract or something.

Each hotel had its own gangster sort of boss. The

hotel guests and the gamblers thought it was part of the local color. It was a sinful town, and these were the guys in charge. It was sort of romantic.

Which was possible, because unlike the gangster bosses in Chicago, or New York, or Cleveland, these guys didn't air their dirty laundry in their own town. Part of the deal was, you couldn't do anything bad in Las Vegas. The gangsters were not gangster gangsters. It was a free zone. You could not do anything here. You couldn't kill anyone here, or anything. When they had to do any kind of killing, it had to be done in Arizona, or somewhere else out in the desert. So it was easier to think of them as romantic characters.

There's still some of that old Las Vegas around. If you know where to look. For example, all the *Sopranos* guys went out to see Tom Jones sing. There was twelve of us, and he comped the whole group. It was a brilliant show. Best in town. He's got the pipes.

And every night, after the show, he goes to dinner someplace, at midnight. He takes along a bunch of people. He'll drink and he'll eat and he'll sing. See, that's the deal. He has someone call ahead to make sure that he can eat and drink all he wants, he and all his friends, for free—if he agrees to sing. It's good for business, right. The restaurants always say yes. Who doesn't want

Tom Jones eating dinner and singing in their joint? It's like a taste of the real old Las Vegas.

Some other things a goomba will never say:

Sure you can have my Social Security number.
No problem, pay me when you have the money.
Mom, don't worry about it. I'll do my own laundry.
I'm trading in my Firebird for a minivan.
I'd love to, sweetheart, but I'm a married man.
Someone should bust up these unions.

The trouble is, it's late. And he's tired. He's no kid. And he's been onstage for hours. So, he wants to have a few drinks and a few laughs, and then he wants something to eat. And by the time he's ready to sing for his supper, you know, it's like four o'clock in the morning. And now he's had a few cocktails, and he's *really* tired. Most of the other customers have given up and gone home, but the owner's pissed—'cause he's bought dinner and drinks for fifteen people. So it's five o'clock in the morning, and the owner's, like, "He's gotta sing."

He always sings, but by the time he does, everyone's too tired to care.

~ ~ ~

OF COURSE NOT all goombas who get on the wrong side of the law are gangsters. Other guys are just goomba criminals. I knew about these two guys in Vegas, for example. They were into drugs. Cocaine. They were drug dealers. They sold a lot of cocaine—so much that they got the attention of the cops. They had reason to believe that the cops had them under surveillance, listening to them on a wire tap. But they didn't want to stop dealing. (Apparently there was a lot of money in that line of work.) So they developed a code language for their business. A gram of cocaine, say, was "a pair of pants." Two grams was "two pairs of pants."

Things went along pretty good for them. They were moving a lot of merchandise and making a lot of money. One guy would say, "I'd like to order three pairs of pants." The other guy would say, "Your three pairs of pants are ready. I'm having them sent over."

The cops were listening, the whole time, but what are they gonna do? You can't arrest a guy for buying a pair of pants.

But the goombas got too smart. They thought their system was foolproof. They thought the cops wouldn't figure it out. Now they got a big order. They're excited.

So one of them says to the other, "I'm gonna need three and a half pairs of pants."

Three and a half pairs of pants!

That was the end of it. The goombas were arrested and sent to jail.

This is the kind of thing that can happen to goombas when they get too far from home; a goomba that's not too bright can end up in over his head.

In the old days, in the neighborhood, things were different. The neighborhood was controlled by a family. The family was controlled by the godfather—some people called him the *padrone*. The *padrone* kept everyone in line. There wasn't any crime in his neighborhood. He looked out for his people. People came to him with their problems, and he gave them assistance.

For example, when my friend Mikey's dad got laid off, the *padrone* got him a job tending bar in one of the mob joints. Later, he got him a job driving a bread truck. Was he really delivering bread? Who knows? But the godfather was looking out for Mikey's dad, and his family, even though he was not in any way connected to the mob. He was just a guy from the neighborhood who was having a hard time.

Those days are pretty much over.

Sometimes you'll still people hear say, "That neighborhood is the safest neighborhood in New York because those people take care of things." They're talking about this part of Brooklyn or that part of Staten Island where the neighborhood is still controlled by a family. They think the old rules still apply.

In one section I could tell you about, there was never any assaults or murders, for years. Then one day these two Puerto Rican kids tried to grab an old lady's purse. She screamed, and the kids took off, and people started screaming. The kids ran right in front of one of

Uncle Danny must have hit the wrong note.

the local "social clubs." Bad luck for them. Some of the boys came outside and caught one of them. The local boss asks what's going on. The boys tell him it's a purse-snatching job. The boss takes one look at the Puerto Rican kid and says, "String 'em up."

There's never been any crime in that neighborhood since. Nobody's stealing any purses around there. Ain't that wonderful? Sure, if you're not the Puerto Rican kid.

Today, when I run into these guys who live like that, it's no different than if I'm running into somebody else. It's just like we're still playing stickball together. They're just guys from the neighborhood. I don't know what they do—but I *know* what they do—and I don't ask and they don't tell. It's not my business. I see them, we hang out, we have a drink, we joke about the old days, about who's doing this and who's doing that. And that's it. The rest is none of my business.

But some of them have very strong opinions about my work on *The Sopranos*. Most of them love the show—all wise guys love this show. It's about them, and they love it. And why not? Tony Soprano is this very charismatic guy. He's strong and he's in charge, most of the time, and he sits around his own nightclub, surrounded by his friends, drinking booze and flirting with chicks and making wisecracks. Who wouldn't like that? If that's all there was to being a gangster, I'd probably be one myself. Of course that's just one tiny aspect of it. The rest of it ain't such a picnic.

Chapter 3

GOOMBA LOVE
... AND BEYOND

These goomba guys,

they know how

to treat a girl nice.

You might not automatically connect the idea of love and the idea of goomba, but the goomba is a very romantic guy. Love is important to him—love with the opposite sex, love with his family, love with his children. Goomba love is very strong. The goomba ain't fickle. He may be a married guy who fools around on the side, but when it comes to the people he really loves . . . it's *forever*. A goomba never forgets, and a goomba never changes his mind. For his friends, for his wife, for his parents and his children, goomba love is permanent.

I don't know if my own story is representative or not, but I'm gonna tell parts of it in the hope that it illustrates the goomba way of love.

I was fifteen when I lost my virginity. On the golf course. That was how it was done in my neighborhood.

See, there was this golf course in the neighborhood. That's where you'd take the girls to make out. You'd say, "You wanna take a walk down by the golf course?" And they knew what that meant. You were going to go down to the golf course and make out—and maybe go a little further. You'd go down there with your goomba girl, and that was that.

That year a couple of my friends had already done it and I wanted to do it, too. So one of them set me up. He had lost his virginity with a girl named I Love Lucy. She had red hair and a big mouth, like Lucille Ball. This guy—he's a cop now, his name is Anthony—set me up with I Love Lucy. And we went walking.

It was horrible. It was right in the middle of the summer. It was hot and sticky, and there were a billion mosquitoes. We started in on the golf course, and it got pretty hot and heavy, and pretty soon I've got my pants off, and away we go. It's me and the mosquitoes. It was so bad, no kidding, that I couldn't even finish. I had to get up and move. We ended up in an abandoned car.

The next day I was so proud. I wanted to tell the boys, to show off, and let everyone know. And the best way to show that I had lost my virginity was the mosquito bites. So I dropped my pants and they started counting. I had twenty-five mosquito bites on my ass! They counted! It was proof. I was in the club.

I saw Anthony recently and we were joking about it. He said, "Remember when you nailed I Love Lucy?" We laughed about it. I have no idea what happened to I Love Lucy.

So much for my romantic notions—the beach, the moonlight! Not for me. I got mosquitoes and an abandoned car.

When I was growing up, dating was not like today. First of all, it wasn't really dating. You knew everybody from the neighborhood. You knew everyone's family, and everyone's father, and everyone's brothers and cousins. It wasn't like you were just going to hit on someone and ask them out.

My mom and dad on their honeymoon. Where else? The Poconos.

Instead, you'd sort of decide on someone, and you'd ask them, "So, you wanna go out with me?" After that, if she said yes, you were *with* her. Everyone knew. And then you'd go out.

There was a big group of us, maybe twenty-five or thirty guys. And we all had our girlfriends. If you went to a party, or a wedding, or a funeral, or a New Year's party, that's who you saw. Saturday night, we'd all go out together—big groups sometimes, smaller groups sometimes. You'd go to a restaurant, or a nightclub, or maybe a bar. On Friday night, all the guys from the group would get together. And all the girls from the group would get together, too. That's the tradition, again. Friday night, you mess around. Saturday night is for wives—or the girlfriends, before they become the wives.

The sex thing was a little difficult, because in those days no one lived together before they got married, and everyone lived at home. There was none of this shacking up. And no one had an apartment or anything. You lived with your parents, usually, until you got married. So, you spent a lot of time in hotel rooms.

That was hard for me, because I didn't have a lot of money. In those days there weren't any hotels in Brooklyn, so we had to go to Jersey, and even the cheap hotels were twenty-two bucks a day, which in those days was a lot of money to us.

So I had a little scheme. I'd drive over to Jersey and pick up a pizza and a six-pack of beer, and I'd check in to the Benedict Hotel. It was twenty-two bucks a day. It would take forty-five minutes or so to drive over there. I'd check in around noon. I'd stay in the room until six o'clock. Then I'd pay the maid three bucks to clean the room, and I'd drive back to Brooklyn, and give the key to a buddy of mine so he could take the late shift. Then he'd split the twenty-two bucks with me.

That was a date. That was a night out. Otherwise, if you were flush, maybe you'd have a few drinks and dinner first, and then you'd go to the hotel and not have to split the twenty-two bucks. That was dating.

But you had to watch out, growing up where I did, who you dated. Some wise guy's niece, or his daughter . . . you didn't want that. You take a girl like that out and bring her home at five o'clock in the morning? You'd wind up with a baseball bat cracking your head open. This was an occupational hazard of growing up in a goomba neighborhood. No mob guy wants his daughter or his niece going out with some slug from the corner. And if you were the slug . . . it was gonna get ugly.

When you did date, you stayed pretty close to home. In general, Italians stick to Italians. Most goombas, they don't get around much. The guys from my neighborhood definitely didn't get around too much—going to Manhattan was a huge thing. We might as well have lived in another state. Everybody stuck to the neighborhood. Which meant that the goomba guys wound up with goomba girls. Goombettes.

These girls, they're like gun molls. They're like gangster chicks. Some of them, they got a mouth like a truck driver. They're very tough. They tell you exactly what's what—what's on their mind, how they feel, what they want. There's no fooling around. There's no hinting around. There's none of this touchy-feely, marriage-encounter, "relationship" business. It's right out there. You're doing something wrong, you're going to hear about it.

Same thing with the goomba guys. They can be very blunt—and some girls like that. With a goomba, you know exactly where they're at. If a guy likes you, you know right away that he's interested. You know where he's coming from. And it can be very romantic. These goomba guys, they know how to treat a girl nice. They know the best restaurants, and they get the best tables, and they're not afraid to throw some dough around. It's very old fashioned, and it can be very charming.

Not that it's all love and romance. There's other stuff, too.

Some guys I know went with hookers. When they wanted sex, they'd seek professional help. In fact, one of my friends had a sort of goomba gimmick with hookers. He and six of his friends would go over to this town where they knew the hookers hung out. And this guy would go talk to the hooker. He was the smooth-talker in the bunch, the one with all the charm, and he'd do the negotiating. He'd go over and take the hooker aside, like into a storefront, and he'd make the deal—while all his buddies waited in the car.

What they didn't know was this smooth-talking friend of mine always made a side deal for himself. If the guys had fifty bucks, he'd make the deal for all six of them to go with the hooker for eight bucks each. But he got to go first, and for free. His friends never knew that he wasn't paying.

On the other hand, I knew another bunch of guys who decided to rob a hooker. They had this brilliant plan to go into Manhattan and grab a hooker and take her money. Geniuses. So they go into Manhattan, and they pick up a hooker, but she's smarter than they are. An hour later, they're pissed—'cause they paid ten bucks a piece for blow jobs. So they had to grab another hooker. This time they got the purse, which had a comb, some coins, and some multi-colored condoms. Everybody knows a hooker doesn't carry cash in her purse, but not these goombas. They weren't your smart goombas.

In goomba relationships, whether it's people dating or people married, there are some things a goomba will never say. Here are a few:

I just want a woman I can open up to.
Honey, those pants are too tight, and the heels are too tall.
Can't we just cuddle?
My fiancée insists on a small wedding.
Our favorite movie? *On Golden Pond.*
Sex is wonderful, but I crave intimacy.
Real women don't have fake breasts.
I think sexy lingerie makes a woman look cheap.

THE GOOMBA MARRIAGE

ROMANCE ASIDE, there's a lot of tradition in goomba marriages—and a lot of hypocrisy. It ain't that way in my house, but that's how it is in some families.

For example. I got this friend, a real goomba, who works in a casino. He's got a wife and a couple of kids, and he screws around with hookers. No big thing, he's happily married! But then he meets someone, and he falls in love. He's married, but this is the love of his life!

And she's married, too. She tells her husband that she's in love with someone else. She tells my friend that he's got to tell his wife. But he can't.

One day he comes home from work, and there's his wife, sitting on the sofa, talking to his girlfriend. They're having the whole discussion. The girlfriend says, "He loves me. You don't even sleep with him anymore." The wife says, "Yeah, not since Wednesday."

So the girlfriend tells the wife about the hookers.

My friend is dying here.

Finally the wife says, "My father cheated on my mother. My grandfather cheated on my grandmother. You do what you need to do, you bum." She kicks him out.

He went with the girlfriend. Guess what? It didn't work out.

Two weeks later, he was back with his wife. That was ten years ago. They're still together.

That's pretty much a typical goomba marriage. Look at *The Sopranos*. Carmela knows Tony has a girl-friend. She smells it on his shirt. But she accepts it—as long as he comes home at night, and pays the bills, and takes care of his family. That's enough.

So, a lot of guys, they got something on the side. We even have a word for it—"goomah," or "goomar,"

or "comare." If you take it literally it means god-
mother, but to the goomba it means mistress—steady
girlfriend, for a goomba guy.

All the mob guys I knew, growing up, they had a
goomar. They'd keep the girls in an apartment, buy 'em
stuff, keep 'em quiet. And then on Friday night, they'd
take them out—to a club, to a show, for drinks and dinner. Never on a Saturday. Saturday night is for wives.
You take your wife out on Saturday night. Friday night
is for the girlfriend.

That doesn't mean a goomba doesn't love his wife.
A goomba is a family man. He loves his family more
than anything. It's just not, like, exclusive. He might be
a very loving guy. He might have a lot of love to give.
So, he might need an extra person to give it to. That's
your goomar.

Sometimes, even a solid goomba marriage can fall
apart. Take my pal Angelo, for example. His wife was a
wedding singer. She'd do weddings every weekend, and
he always went along to watch.

Now, his wife is a real looker. And Angelo, he's jeal-
ous. A lot of times, at the weddings, guys start flirting
with the wedding singer. That's natural. She's beautiful, and she's singing romantic songs . . . It's gotta
happen.

But Angelo can't take it. So one time, his wife is

singing, and some guy has had a little too much to drink, and when she comes past his table singing her song, he grabs her and pulls her down into his lap. Angelo goes nuts. He goes after the guy, he's got him on the floor, and he's choking him to death! The wedding is ruined! His wife's career is ruined!

So she leaves him. She files for divorce. Angelo is a wreck. He's a goomba with a broken heart. He rides the train for three days. He don't know what to do! He can't go home to his wife. He can't go home to his mother. So he sends his wife a note. He tells her he will wait for her, in front of the movie theater, on Wednesday night, at eight o'clock. He says he'll wait for her every Wednesday night, until she forgives him.

For six months, he waits! How's that for love? So romantic! So dedicated! What a goomba!

Unfortunately, she never comes.

Finally Angelo gave up. Luckily, he got remarried.

As for me, I been married a long time. In this area, I may not be your typical goomba, but I don't fool around. Don't want to. Don't need to. I got all the love I can handle right at home. Maybe that makes me different. But I think it makes me a better goomba. An enlightened goomba. A sort of New Age goomba, a goomba for the millennium, if you will.

For Richer, For Poorer

For better or worse, the goomba's gonna get married eventually. He wants a family, he wants the kids, maybe he wants the goomar. You can't have a mistress if you don't have a wife. So he gets a wife.

Once he's got the family, he's the man of the house. And for the man in the goomba house, the best day of the week is Sunday.

A DAY IN THE GOOMBA LIFE

THE GOOMBA LOVES Sunday. I love Sunday. Sunday is the great day—the favorite day of the week for your goomba. Friday night is fun. Saturday night there's always something going on. But Sunday is the best.

First of all, the goomba gets up late on a Sunday morning. He rolls out of bed, wearing boxer shorts and a guinea T-shirt and black socks. That's like goomba pajamas.

Mrs. Goomba is waiting. She's got coffee and the newspaper, which no one has touched. No one reads the paper before the man of the house.

He goes right to the sports section. This may be all he reads, but he always reads the sports section. And the first thing he does is check the number. He's prob-

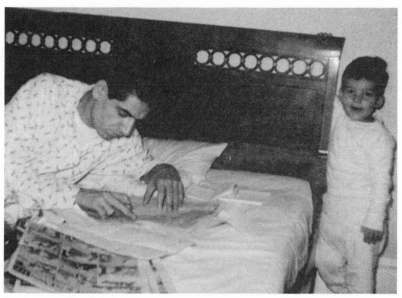

My dad, checking the number. Me, just hanging out.

ably playing the number. Everybody in the neighborhood plays the number—the old ladies, the young men, everyone. Maybe he's laid down a few bucks. Probably nothing big—ten bucks, maybe. Still, he's got to know.

The number is a three-digit number. You pick your favorite. Some people, it changes all the time. Other people, it's always the same. But it's a three-digit number. And the winning number is always determined the same way, and announced the same way. It's the last three numbers in the total mutuel handle from one of the local race tracks—and the total mutuel handle is the total amount of money wagered at the track on the previous day. So, say the number is set by the handle at Aquaduct, and say the total amount of money wagered at that race track the day before was $1,786,309. Then 309 is the number.

If you hit the number, it's payday. From Harlem to Canal Street, every day, someone is celebrating. My father hit the number many a time when I was a kid, and it was like Christmas every time.

But usually the goomba doesn't win. That's okay. He's got breakfast coming.

It's a Sunday, remember, and Sunday is a big day for food. So the goomba is not going to have a big meal for his breakfast. He's gonna eat kinda light. He's gonna have eggs, sunny side up, toast, a little bacon— nothing crazy. Maybe he likes pepperoni for breakfast, so he gets pepperoni and eggs. A light meal. A little provolone with his eggs. Some nice Italian bread, buttered. Coffee. Nice. Not too heavy. Maybe a little dessert afterwards.

Then he gets cleaned up, and has a shower and a shave. He's going to put on a jogging suit. If he's going to have people coming in, he'll put on a "nice" jogging suit. He'll put on his jewelry—the pinky rings, the watch, the bracelets, and the gold chains (which he's already wearing, because he sleeps in those)—and splash on a little Drakkar aftershave.

By now, the football game is on, so the TV's going. The goomba has laid down a few bets, so he's watching the games. He might call his bookie and put in a few more bets. And maybe people are starting to arrive.

Sunday, you never have visitors. No friends. Sunday is family. But the goomba's got a big family, so by the middle of the day, there's people over. Maybe some cousins and nephews. They're sitting watching the game. All of the men are in the living room, watching the game. All of the women are in the kitchen, talking and cooking. There's no mixing here.

The men are probably having a beer by now, too. But nothing fancy. Nothing imported. The average goomba drinks an average beer—maybe a Budweiser. Don't give the goomba any fancy crap. None of that Sam Adams. None of the Heineken.

There's always music playing. So the game is on, but so is some nice goomba music. Maybe it's Tony Bennett or Al Martino. Or maybe Lou Monte. Lou Monte! He was always on *The Ed Sullivan Show*. We had all his records. He sang, "Peppino, You Little Italian Mouse," and "Lazy Mary." What a singer. "Peppino, oh you little mouse, oh won't you run away . . ." Every Italian loves this! It's a goomba classic.

They're having a snack, too. Mrs. Goomba is cooking Sunday sauce, so she's got sausage and meatballs going. So maybe she makes a little tray of fried meat-balls. Maybe a little cheese. Maybe some little sausages. Just a snack. She'll bring this out on a tray for the men to eat while they watch the game. Maybe a little bread with this. Maybe sometimes a little homemade pizza or focaccia bread. Nothing heavy. Remember, the big meal is coming, so these are just appetizers to get the goomba through the day until his dinner arrives.

Dinner's at two o'clock. In some households, that would be early. But in the goomba household, you have to eat early. Otherwise, you won't have time to eat twice—and the goomba family has to eat twice on Sunday. First you eat dinner, and then after resting a few hours you eat dinner again. It's tradition!

Here comes dinner. It's a typical huge meal. You start with antipast'. It's a big tray of salami and pep-peroni and tomatoes and peppers and olives and maybe some mixed greens. This comes with a nice Italian bread with good crust. There's going to be some marinated vegetables with this, maybe some asparagus or cauliflower. Maybe there's some grilled vegetables, too—roasted peppers in oil or grilled eggplant.

Next comes the macaroni. Sunday sauce on rigatoni is always nice. Penne alla vodka. Maybe it's a lasagna. Maybe it's some manicotti. It's a big plate of macaroni,

My dad presides over Sunday dinner.

whatever it is. This gets passed around, and everyone is twirling spaghetti and dipping the bread in the sauce. There's not too much talking by now. The goombas are busy eating. There's a lot of food to get through. You have to pace yourself and concentrate. You can't be gulping air or yacking too much, or swallowing too much wine or soda. You gotta just sit quietly and eat, if you want to enjoy it properly.

That's because the main course hasn't even arrived yet. The macaroni may be the main course in a non-goomba household. It may be the main part of the dinner on another night of the week in a goomba household. But on Sunday, it's just the macaroni. It ain't the whole dinner.

On Sunday, you've got a roast beef coming—at least. Maybe it's a nice veal roast, or maybe a veal chop, or a chicken. Maybe it's a big osso bucco. Whatever it is, it's some kind of meat, and there's a lot of it. Some of the goombas are going to want second helpings. You gotta be sure there's enough for that. This is the most important part of the meal. If you don't have enough of the roast, someone's gonna say, "Nice dinner. What are we, on a diet?" Never mind they already ate enough to feed a small village.

Everyone eats. Everyone drinks—red wine, now, with the meal. After, there's a nice espresso, with some cannoli or an Italian cheesecake.

Then the goomba takes a nap. He's gotta rest. Because at six o'clock they're gonna break out the food again for round two. So the goomba needs a rest.

There's not much other activity on Sunday. Your goomba dad might play catch with his son. He might go into the yard and look around a little. Maybe he tends his garden a little—'cause that's his hobby, along with playing the horses and yelling at his wife. Maybe he's growing tomatoes and some basil. He grows stuff for his sauce.

But he's not doing much else. The goomba Sunday does not include any sporting activity. The goomba ain't playing golf or tennis—not Sunday, not any day. He's not at the gym. He's not swimming any laps. He's not playing touch football. None of that suburban white-bread action. He *watches* things like that. He doesn't indulge personally.

Training in Bensonhurst. Uncle Freddy, 1947.

And he doesn't do any physical labor—ever, if at all possible—and he certainly never does any on a Sunday. The goomba is not working on his car on a Sunday. He is not mowing the lawn. He is *not* going shopping with his wife—not Sunday, not ever. The only heavy lifting he's doing today is eating. So he's reserving all his energy for that.

Years later, living in Las Vegas, I try to have that kind of Sunday all over again. I got friends over, and my family around me, and we have just the sort of goomba Sunday I remember from when I was a kid. Some of the people that come for Sunday dinner are goombas.

Some of them are not. They might not be Italian at all. But they all like the Sunday dinner. Who wouldn't? It's restful and civilized, and involves mainly eating, talking, watching a ball game and napping. Most guys feel very reassured when they realize no one is mowing the goomba lawn on Sunday. There ain't gonna be no chores. No one's strapping on the tool belt or going out to the garage to finish sanding shelves for that armoire. There's no leaky pipes getting fixed.

And there's no sports to play either. There's not gonna be any sweating. No touch football game in the backyard. No pick-up basketball game. No sports.

Every culture has some kind of tradition worth saving. This is one of the goomba traditions I'm hoping to pass on to my kids. Maybe if more families sat down on a Sunday and had this kind of day to themselves, they'd all be happier families.

THE GOOMBA ON VACATION

A LOT OF goombas from the neighborhood don't have regular jobs. So they don't go on regular vacations. Every day is a vacation. You look at the average goomba's daybook—I mean, if he *had* a daybook, which he doesn't—and it reads like a guy already on vacation.

Monday: Lunch with Vinnie. Tuesday: Lunch with Frankie. Wednesday: Lunch with Sally. Thursday: Drinks with Vito.

But if he goes on vacation, he's going to Vegas or Florida or maybe the Bahamas. That's it. There isn't anyplace else. The goomba ain't no tourist. He is not going sightseeing. He's not going to Niagara Falls or San Francisco. The Grand Canyon ain't on the list. The goomba is not going to Mt. Rushmore or Yellowstone National Park.

He's going to a place where he can relax and he's not going alone, either. Goombas travel in packs. The goomba takes the wife, and they go with two or three other couples. And wherever they are—Ft. Lauderdale, Miami, Caesars Palace, whatever—it's the same. If it's during the day, they're at the pool. They're working on that tan, because you gotta come home with a tan. They're drinking that piña colada, which is a classic goomba drink. The wives are wearing bikinis. The goomba is wearing baggy shorts. You won't find a goomba in a Speedo. Maybe an Italian, but never a goomba. That's for sissies.

At night, the goomba is going to do it right. He'll have a nap in the afternoon, of course. And after that he'll put on some nice slacks and one of those Tommy Bahama shirts—like a big Hawaiian shirt, you know,

Who said we don't play tennis? Me and the guys in 1977.

but without the flowers and trees and stuff. And he'll take the wife to a show, and to dinner, and to drinks. He'll do it up. If they're in Vegas, he'll hit the tables a little. Play a little blackjack. Play a little craps. Nothing heavy. He's on vacation, remember?

Gambling, for the goomba, is not some special, once-in-a-lifetime deal. He's probably got a poker game at home, and he's playing the horses all the time, and he's playing the numbers, and he's betting on sports. So the gambling isn't a big deal to him.

Unless he has a problem. Some people do. During the time I worked in Las Vegas, I saw plenty of that. I saw people, good goombas, even, come out and lose everything. I once saw a guy not even make it to his

See? I was skinny once. Florida, 1977.

room. He was checking in, and they told him he'd have to wait a while for the room to be made ready. The bell-man got his bags, and he went over to kill some time at the craps table. He lost everything in a couple of hours. He never made it to his room. They brought his bags back down and got him a cab to the airport.

Another time, a friend of mine, a good goomba guy, he went to Vegas on his honeymoon. He sends the wife up to the room to get freshened up. He wants to give her some time to herself, so he stays downstairs in the casino. And he goes nuts. He starts losing, and he can't stop. Pretty soon he's gone through all the vacation money, and all the wedding present money. He's got nothing left to pay for the room, or a meal, or even a phone call. The management gets his wife to come downstairs. This is in the old days, and these people were from the neighborhood, remember, so they've never lived together or nothing like that. So they leave Las Vegas, these newlyweds, without even consummating the marriage! Going home, broke.

The average goomba, though, he's just there to have some fun, and he will. He knows how to get a good table, and get tickets for the right show. Maybe he's going to see Tom Jones or Johnny Mathis. In the old days, of course, it was all Sinatra, and Dean Martin, and Sammy Davis Jr. The wife is all dolled up. She's got the big hair, and the tight pants, or the tight dress. She's wearing her jewelry. She's got twenty pounds of make-up on. Beautiful!

The goomba knows how to have a good time. He may not know how to order a good wine, but he knows how to tell the waiter to *bring* him a good wine. And if he's throwing around a little money, he'll get a good wine. If he gets up to go to the men's room, he'll even have a nice time in there.

Goombas love the men's room. They love the attendants and all that stuff. They know how to *enjoy* that stuff. They'll come in and take a leak, and they'll let the attendant run the whisk broom over their jacket. They'll take a splash of the cologne, maybe take a swig of the mouthwash. Use the hairbrushes or the combs. Pat themselves dry with a little towel. Maybe buff up the shoes a little. The average goomba could spend fifteen minutes just freshening up. He's worse than a woman!

Years ago, when I worked at Paul Anka's place, there was a men's room attendant there named Howard. Howard the Toilet Man. Howard ran that place like it was his own home. He was there, night and day. He had been some kind of a goomba in Chicago, and his business had gone bust, so he'd come out west to make his fortune—like the rest of us. This was the best he could do.

The mob guys were still in town then. Tony Spilotro and Lefty Rosenthal were still running things. And they'd come in all the time. Howard the Toilet Man knew their habits. Howard knew how often they'd come in to piss. He'd say, "Tony, he's good for two-three shots a night." Two or three times a night, that meant two or three tips a night. So he knew what he was going to get from each guy.

It was an art form with him. He took his work very seriously. Howard would stand there, brushing a guy off with a whisk broom *while he's taking a leak.* It was the ultimate toilet hustle. A guy brushes you off while you're taking a leak, you gotta give him a couple of bucks! Howard was clearing $300 a night. He was sort of a celebrity. Like the maitre d' of the toilet. I remember him showing me once what he'd got from Bob Hope, who was just leaving the can when I was walking in. Bob Hope! A quarter and a nickel! From Bob Hope. And Howard was getting tens and twenties from mob guys. He'd give 'em gum, and he'd give 'em cologne, and he'd agree with everything that everybody said. That was his thing. The conversation would go like this:

GUY 1: "That guy Johnny, what a pain in the ass."
HOWARD: "Unbelievable! What a jerk!"
GUY 2: "Johnny? What's wrong with Johnny? He's a great guy."
HOWARD: "I *love* Johnny."

Bottom line? Your goomba likes to have things just so, whether he's at home or on vacation—or in the men's room. He wants to have a good time and be treated nice. And hey, what's wrong with that?

Chapter 4

GOOMBA
ETIQUETTE

Just be careful
who you tip.
Cops, for example,
you never tip.

S top laughing. Goomba etiquette ain't one of those oxymorons—you know, like military intelligence or jumbo shrimp. Goomba etiquette is a real thing. There are rules and right ways to do things. There are definitely wrong things to do, too. Most goombas grow up just knowing how to behave properly in the goomba world. But to outsiders, the whole thing probably looks confusing. How do you dress? What do you order in a restaurant? How do you tip? Who do you tip, and how much? What do you take to a goomba wedding? What do you say at a goomba funeral? This chapter will answer some of those questions.

This chapter will also show the reader how he can behave like a stand-up guy even if he's not a goomba—or even if he's not in a goomba predicament. These are pretty good rules for living in general. Just be careful who you tip. Cops, for example, you never tip. Same with judges. Same with doctors. You always wait, with those guys, until they *ask* for the money . . .

THE GOOMBA WEDDING

WEDDINGS AND FUNERALS are a huge part of goomba life. Every one of them is like a huge reunion. Everyone comes—all the family, all the friends, and they stay forever. A wedding will start in the afternoon, in the church, and it will go until almost the next morning. They're very expensive, these weddings. If you're the goomba father-of-the-bride, it's a point of honor to have the best wedding possible for your daughter. No expense is spared—the dress, the outfits for the brides-maids, the decorating of the hall, the food, the music . . . Nothing but the best will do.

Here's the weird part. Unlike weddings in other cultures, money actually changes hands at a goomba wedding. No one brings a toaster to a goomba wedding. No goomba bride is registered at Macy's or Crate and Barrel. At a true goomba wedding, it's all *cash*. The family has spent a small fortune putting the wedding on, and the guests better come with cash, too.

This money is called the *a boost*. Everyone brings the *a boost*. You gotta come with the *a boost*. You show up without the *a boost*, forget it. You might as well go home. You're not welcome.

You saw it in the movie *GoodFellas*. The new bride has this beaded bag, and people are at it with money. The rich goombas, the big gangster bosses, they're putting lots of money in there. The poor goombas, they're putting less money in there. But everyone has an envelope to stuff in the beaded bag. At other goomba weddings, there's a receiving line. Each of the guests comes up and congratulates the bride and groom, and gives up the *a boost*.

And most goombas know, going in, how much the *a boost* has gotta be. If it's a wedding, or a funeral, or whatever, you gotta come with the *a boost*. This is how it goes:

"What's the date?"
"It's Saturday."
"This Saturday? I gotta give the *a boost*?"
"Of course the *a boost*. Whatta you think?"
"Alright, alright. How much?"
"A couple hundred."

Here's how you figure the amount. First you try to calculate the cost of the meal. If it's just a so-so wedding, maybe the dinner is $100 a head. So you wanna give about $200 in the *a boost*. My wife and I go to a wedding, we figure the dinner is $200 a person, we're gonna give $500 or $600.

You'll hear people complain sometimes. "I hardly know the guy, and he wants me to come to his wedding? He's only inviting me for the *a boost*."

A cheap goomba like that has been known to make a withdrawal from the *a boost* while he's already at the wedding. Many a cheap goomba has been overheard, saying he didn't think the wedding was all that nice, taking a hundred out of his envelope before he gives the *a boost*. This is bad goomba behavior, but you see it just the same.

I got married in Las Vegas, but ours wasn't a one-hundred-percent goomba wedding. How do I know? I got toasters. Some of the guests didn't understand about the *a boost*. Maybe nobody told them. So they brought a toaster. When my wedding was over, I had about $15,000 in cash, four toasters, and a blender or two. I think we took the appliances out in the desert and buried them.

The typical goomba wedding, it's a huge affair. Everyone has to be invited. Many a family feud has been started when some goomba cousin or aunt was

My mother and father's wedding, 1949.

left out. So, you got maybe four hundred or five hundred people coming. It's going to be at the catering hall. Some of the nice ones are in Staten Island. Some are in Jersey, or on the water in Long Island. And it ain't cheap. I've been to weddings that cost $100,000. And please remember, these are not rich people throwing these weddings. These are working-class goomba people, having working-class goomba weddings. The father of the bride is a policeman, or a fireman, or a garbage man, or a plumber.

The church part of the wedding lasts forever. Figure an hour for the Mass alone. So as soon as the reception starts, it's the cocktail hour. And this part alone is like most dinners at a regular wedding. There's baked clams and lobster claws, and all kinds of shrimp. There's eggplant parmesan and meatballs, and sausages and peppers. And lots of fresh cheese. There's a whole buffet of the stuff. I've been to non-goomba weddings where the dinner wasn't as elaborate as the cocktail-hour part of the goomba wedding. Because this isn't even the dinner yet.

The bride and groom, they're not around during the cocktail hour. They're downstairs or upstairs, partying with the bridesmaids and ushers. They've already been partying plenty. The bridesmaids have had the shower a week or more ago, and they've given out the gag gifts like the vibrators along with the sensible stuff. And the groom has had his bachelor party, which consists of drinks, dinner, and some strippers. Maybe a hooker for some of the guys. (Not for me, thanks, but some goombas go that way.) Sometimes things get carried away. I went to one wedding where the groom and all the ushers had black eyes. They got into a scrape at the bachelor party, the Friday night before the Sunday wedding, and they all had to fight their way out. The wedding pictures are beautiful!

When the couple finally makes the big entrance the band is playing the couple's favorite song. It's a big band. They're making $6,000 to $10,000 for the night, playing Top 40 and Motown and disco.

After the big entrance everyone sits down for dinner. Now it's time for the big food. No lasagna; we're talking steak and veal and lobster and chicken. Shrimp cocktail. Some kind of salad. It's gonna be a good meal, and the food is gonna go on a long time. The reception might have started at six. Now it's nine, and you're just finishing dinner. Then it's the Venetian Hour. Don't ask me why it's called that, but the waiters come with every kind of dessert you ever saw. Baked Alaska. Pies. Cakes. Ice cream. Espresso. Sambucca.

There's not much speaking at the goomba wedding. There's no roasting the bride and groom—we're too busy eating. The couple gets introduced as Mr. and Mrs. Goomba for the first time. Then the bride has to dance with her father, to "Daddy's Little Girl." Everyone has to cry a little now. Very sweet. Everyone applauds, everyone cries.

Then the bride throws the bouquet. It's always the fat goomba cousin that catches it, the one with the big moustache. She's never getting married, so what the hell? The groom pulls off the garter. All that stuff.

Then comes the *a boost*. The bride and the groom sit

on the dais. The reception line forms. Everyone comes
with the money. Sometimes it's in special envelopes.
Money envelopes, or money cards, with a cut-out place
to put the money. That way, you look in and, Hello! It's
Benjamin Franklin. It's Andrew Jackson! You know
how much money is there. And the bride puts the *a
boost* in her little beaded sack. The couple is getting
their big start in life.

When it's all collected, the *a boost* might be half the
cost of the wedding. A $100,000 wedding, you got a
$50,000 *a boost.* It's a downpayment on a house. On the

More goomba giveaways:

- There were more sweatsuits at your uncle's funeral
  than at the Olympics opening ceremony.
- Your father used to give you your allowance out of
  the teamster's pension fund.
- Your satellite dish has the Virgin Mary on it.
- You ever did the Electric Slide next to John Gotti Jr.
- The bumper sticker on your Camaro reads "My other
  car is a Camaro."
- Your grandmother is stopped on the street when
  people mistake her for Tony Siragusa.

other hand, sometimes the father of the bride has to dip into the *a boost* just to pay for the wedding. Many a goomba father has had to stick his hand in there to pay the catering hall.

After the wedding, the bride and groom go to the hotel suite. The next day, probably, they're going to Miami or Honolulu. They might be going to Aruba or Bermuda. Someplace with sun. The goomba honeymoon, you have to come back with a suntan. Otherwise, why did you go? You have to get a suntan.

And that night, of course, the bride and groom also consummate the marriage. To tell the truth, it probably ain't the first time. Maybe in the old days, she would have been a virgin until the wedding night. These days, your goomba is going to test drive the car before he makes the purchase, you know? But remember that both the goombas are probably still living at home, so tonight is the first night they get to stay together, the whole night. That's what makes it special. Goomba love. Very sweet.

Most goomba weddings, there's not a lot of boozing. The wedding doesn't get out of control too often. It's a happy occasion, and every goomba is on his best behavior. This is the day that every goomba girl has been waiting for—for her whole life. This is a classy affair. The goomba is not going to be married by an

Elvis impersonator in some phony chapel. The goomba couple doesn't elope or go to the county courthouse. This is the Big Event.

The day after the big goomba wedding, all the old aunts and grandmothers get together and critique the wedding. Who wore what. Who said what. What about the food. Who gave a big *a boost*. Or, worse, who gave a small *a boost*. There might be gossip about that. A terrible shame for a goomba, to give a cheap *a boost*.

After the honeymoon, they'll live the whole thing over again. There's the wedding pictures, and there's usually the wedding video. They'll get the family together and watch the entire thing, and make jokes, and laugh, and when they play "Daddy's Little Girl," and watch the bride dance again with her father, they'll all cry some more. They'll probably watch the instant replay one more time. And cry some more. Very sentimental, your average goomba.

THE GOOMBA FUNERAL

AFTER HIS WEDDING, the funeral is the other big event in the goomba's life. It's a big part of goomba culture—the other end of the social spectrum from the goomba wedding. Everyone comes. You see all the same people that you saw at your wedding, or your cousin's wedding, or your uncle's funeral. Weddings and funerals, that's where everyone meets.

The typical goomba funeral is a huge event. Between the burial and the wake and the funeral home visits and all the rest, it goes on for days. And it's a big deal for the wives, like a night out! A funeral in the middle of the week is a jackpot for the goomba wife. She gets to dress up, go out, see friends, gossip with her relatives, go to a restaurant, maybe have a few drinks— all in the middle of the week! It's like a holiday. The goomba wives love it.

In my neighborhood, Scarpaci's Funeral Home was where everyone got prepared for burial. The mob guys, the neighborhood guys, the goomba guys—everyone went to Scarpaci in Brooklyn.

The minute you hear someone is at Scarpaci, you start to prepare. People start asking each other, "When's the funeral? Are you going early or late? You wanna eat after? Or before? Where should we eat? You wanna get a couple of drinks before? Or after? Should we meet at Scarpaci, or someplace else?" It's a big event, and you want to do it right.

The rules are pretty strict. You wear black. You act sad. You go in to the funeral home, you sign the book to show you were there, you give a little *a boost* in an envelope, to help pay for the funeral, help out the family, show your respect. You say a few words to the grieving family.

Then you go eat!

Usually you go to the funeral home in the afternoon, and then you go eat. If it's family or someone very close, you go back to the funeral home for a while. If it's done in two rounds, there's always a lot of discussion between this one and that one about how to schedule things. This aunt will call that aunt, and say, "Are you going to eat before or after? Where are you going to eat? Who are you eating with?" Depending on the answer, the two aunts will decide to eat first and go to the funeral home after. Or the other way around. That way, everyone gets together and has a nice afternoon or evening, interrupted, of course, by the sad event of the funeral.

Some people, they're almost professionals. They go to both because they got no life—and because they like funerals. There's a character on *The Sopranos* even, who's *called* "2 to 5, 7 to 9" because she always goes to both. There was a girl from my neighborhood, we called her Fat Pat. She was sort of lonely and she never had a boyfriend, and she started going to funerals. You'd see her at every single funeral. She went to funerals for people she didn't even know. Fat Pat tells the grieving parents, "I'm so sorry. He was such a wonderful man." No one ever questions this. No one says, "Who are you? You didn't even know him!" They thank her and give her a hug. I think she goes just for the hug.

There's also always one person at every funeral who gets hysterical and starts screaming, and then tries to climb into the coffin. I don't know what it is about Italians, or goombas, but this *always* happens. It's almost like they vote, ahead of time. Okay, who's gonna go nuts and climb into the box today? You? You did it last time. Okay, you, then. You go nuts.

At some point in the service, someone starts screaming. "No! No! Take me! I wanna die! Bring him back! Take me instead!" And into the box they go.

I was at one funeral where the man's daughter started screaming about the air conditioning. It was too cold—not for the mourners, you understand, but for her late father. She started screaming, "It's too cold! It's too cold! He's freezing in there!" And then *she* tries to climb into the box.

The goomba, he's a very emotional person. At the goomba funeral, everyone cries. Women, girls, old men, young men, big men and little men, everyone cries! Nothing to be ashamed of. It shows you got heart. Plus it builds up an appetite, so you'll be hungry when you go to dinner after.

Not that it's all tears at a goomba funeral. There are a lot of laughs, too. In Vegas sometimes the funerals felt more like a comedy club than a place of mourning.

There's all kinds of characters running around Las Vegas, and some of them are leftover acts—guys who belonged in Vegas in the '50s or '60s or '70s but who got no place to go now in the new, corporate-run Las Vegas. There's comedians and magicians and singers and dancers and jugglers and mimes, these small-time guys who used to work the clubs and lounges and now they're just starving to death. I still run into them sometimes, but it's usually at a funeral.

I remember once there was a guy who had an act called JTO and Bobby Duck. He had a duck puppet who would sit on his lap and talk dirty and tell jokes. He'd ask the duck, "So, who's your favorite black comic?" And Bobby Duck would say, "Daffy Duck, who else?" That was his big joke. He was becoming very big in Las Vegas until he got diagnosed with cancer; then he was sick a few months, and boom.

At the funeral, it was an open coffin. He's in there, poor JTO, lying in the box, looking peaceful. And right on top of the coffin, I swear, is Bobby Duck—arms stretched out, lying on his back, right there on the mahogany. And all these deadbeat comics are there, hoping to give a little eulogy.

One guy gets up to say a few words, and he does his act. Another guy gets up there and tells jokes. Another guy gets up and plays a kazoo! It's like the lounge from hell! Finally, Sandy Hackett gets up there. He starts doing his act. He's Buddy Hackett's son.

A guy comes over afterwards and says, "Hey, Sandy. Good to see you finally headlining."

HOW TO TIP LIKE A GOOMBA – AND GET WHAT YOU WANT

THIS MIGHT BE the single most mysterious goomba subject. People who don't come from goomba homes find this topic completely confusing. Who do you tip? How do you tip? How much? How much is too much? In fact, it's not that confusing. You just gotta know.

No matter who you are, or where you come from, if you're a goomba you gotta be good with money. You gotta spread it around, if you want to get anywhere. You gotta be a big tipper. This is the only way to get around, the only way to be treated right. You gotta duke 'em. You gotta schmear 'em. You might not be a movie star or a captain of industry, but you can be treated just the same as them if you toss some money around.

Between goombas, tipping and picking up the check is a big thing. Sometimes you gotta fight like hell to get your hands on the check. Everybody wants to be the big man and pay the check, and everybody wants to be the biggest tipper. I've seen guys throw money around at funerals, laying down a big tip just to get a seat close to the coffin. They'll tip the undertaker! I'm joking, but you get the point.

In a restaurant, you tip to get a table. Then you tip to get a better table. You tip to get good service. You give this guy a ten, this guy a twenty, this guy a hundred. If you start throwing around twenties and fifties and hundreds, you're treated like a king, so you feel like a king. You *are* a king.

You tip the valet parking guy. You tip the bartender. You tip your barber. You tip anyone who's gonna remember you and treat you a little better the next time you come in—especially if it's in public, and people are going to *see* you get treated like a king. That's not the point, but it's a little fringe benefit.

In Vegas, the casino employees have a special code for tippers. They say, about a big tipper, "He's George." If there's a big tipper in the house, people working the casino say, "Check him out—the guy's George." You'll hear casino guys talking about someone like he was a celebrity. Maybe they're helping him get a ticket for the fights or for a show. You hear them say, "Can you get a seat for my friend? Don't worry, he's George."

If the guy is a really big tipper, he's "King George." My friend Mikie, who's a craps dealer, he says Dennis Rodman is a King George. (For the record, he also refers to some other basketball players as "Hoardin' Michael Jordan," and "No Tippin' Scotty Pippin.") Mikie says a guy that's an even bigger tipper than a King George is a "King Kong." Larry Flynt, he tells me, is a King George. And Kerry Packer, the financial kingpin from Australia, he's King Kong.

The opposite is too terrible to mention. If you're a stiff, you'll never hear the end of it.

People say, "He's got alligator arms—they don't reach his pockets!"

They say, "He's so cheap, he's still got his communion money."

They say, "He throws quarters around like they were manhole covers."

They say, "This guy don't budge. He ain't coming with nothing."

And that's a disgrace. A real goomba would rather die than let people talk about him that way.

So, here's how it's done—and how it's not done.

The important thing to remember about tipping is this: You're just paying up front for what you want later. It's not about being a big shot or pushing people around. It's not about showing off. It's about asking for a special service and paying for it.

So, what you do is take the money, fold it in half, and discreetly give it to the guy in question and tell him what you need. You're coming into a nightclub for the first time and you want a good seat? You take a twenty, and you say to the maitre d', "I'd like a good seat." If it's an expensive club, or it's really important that you get a good seat, make it a fifty. You say, "How ya doin'?" and you hand him the bill and you say, "I'd like something up in the front."

There's no cat and mouse here. You can't wait and see is the guy going to give you a good seat for nothing. He's not. Getting duked is part of his job. It's how he makes his money. Otherwise, he's getting minimum wage. That seat is how he makes the money to pay his bills. It's not like he's there to make friends. He's not saving the seat for someone he *likes* better than you. He's saving that seat for someone who's throwing him a little bread. You might as well be the guy that gets the good seat. But you gotta pay a little for it.

Maybe you pull into the valet area and the man says, "I'm sorry, but the valet is full." No problem! You're a goomba. You jump out of the car and you say, "That's okay, I'm only going to be about five minutes"—and hand the guy a ten dollar bill. Suddenly the valet ain't so full. The guy can accommodate you after all.

I learned this goomba tipping stuff from my father and later from guys I'd watch in Las Vegas. When my father had a little money, everybody got a little money. He'd spread it around. And he was treated right. Guys in Vegas, it was the same thing. I worked in a nightclub and there was this guy that always came in. He was called "T-Sal." He'd come through the door and hand me $100, and say, "Bring me all the girls you can." He'd order Dom Perignon and sit in a big booth, and I'd send girls to him. I'd tell them, "You wanna drink some Dom and have a few laughs? There's nothing you gotta do for it, but go say hello to T-Sal." He'd get the most beautiful girls sitting and laughing with him. And I'll tell you what: old T-Sal never went home alone. And he wasn't paying for it.

Another guy I knew in Vegas, I'll call him Vito. He was a sort of wiseguy wanna-be. He was a sports gambler, and he made a lot of money. And when he had money, *everybody* had money. I have never seen a white guy throw money around like this guy. He'd hit the bartender with $100, and the maitre d' with $100, and the waiter with $100, and the doorman with $50, and the valet guy with $50. He'd run up a $3,000 tab, drinking champagne and buying people drinks. He'd throw down another $500 in tips. And he was treated like a king—which is interesting, because he was a real jerk, and no one liked him.

These days, since I travel around a lot, I go to a lot of new places. And if I go into a restaurant and I see it's a place I'd like to come back to, I spread around a little money. I'll take good care of the waiter, and especially the bartender, and I'll give the maitre d' and the manager twenty bucks, and the busboy five bucks. I'm not buying anything. I've had my dinner. I don't want anything from them. But I'm coming back, and I'm going to want to be treated right when I do. And I promise you—because it's happened to me time and time again—the next time I come back, and there's a thirty minute wait for a table, I'm not going to be the guy waiting. You'd be amazed how fast you can have a reservation, without making a reservation, if you go to a place where you've spread it around a little.

Not only that, sometimes I'll start the process before I even get there. I'll call to reserve a table, say, and I'll ask the person on the phone to tell me his name or her name. And I'll say, "I'll see you when I get there," or "I'll take care of you when I get there." Then, when I arrive, I make sure to give 'em ten bucks or something.

Just the other day I wanted to take this friend of

mine to a new restaurant that just opened. I don't know anybody over there, so when I called to make the reservation, I asked to speak to the maitre d'. He gets on the phone. He says, "This is Bobby. How can I help you?" I tell him I wanna come in for dinner, and I tell him what time and how many people, and I tell him my name. Bobby repeats the name like we're old friends— and then he repeats *his* name. He thanks me and says, "I'll be here when you arrive. Ask for Bobby."

How easy is that? It's perfect. The guy knows I'm coming, and he knows I'm coming with something for him. I show up, Bobby's waiting, and I slip him a twenty, and he puts us in a beautiful table, and we're watched over like visiting royalty. Instead of sitting at the bar wondering whether we should have tipped someone already.

On the other hand, if you do it wrong, it's ugly. When I was a maitre d', I would sometimes get a kind of show-off tipper. A guy who was a bully with his money. He'd roll up real slow, and take this fat wad of money out of his pocket, and very ceremoniously peel off a hundred dollar bill, and then slap it down on the counter, and say, "Here's a hundred dollars, my friend. Gimme the best seat in the house."

To a guy like that, I'd say, "Sorry, pal. I can't help you."

I don't like being pushed around, not for a hundred dollars, and not by a guy who's that obvious and vulgar about it.

If you're cheap, forget it. It's better not to tip at all than to be a piker. Before he got so famous, the magician David Copperfield used to come into this place where I worked. He'd come over to me and say, "I want you to tell all the girls who I am and send them over to my table." And he'd give me three dollars. Three dollars! He never got any girls from me.

There's no place you can't tip, by the way. In Las Vegas, we have this terrific priest in the Catholic Church. He's the guy that married me and my wife. He was going to do the baptism for my first daughter. It was a big event, you know, with lots of people there. And he did a beautiful job. Afterwards, I took a hundred dollar bill and folded it in half and said, "Father, I want you to have this." I know he doesn't have a lot of money. I wanted to thank him. He said, "No, no. I can't . . ." But his hand came out from under that robe and the money was gone.

A few years later, we're having another baptism, for my second daughter. I've got a scheduling problem. The reception starts at 2:30, and the baptism is at 2:00. I told my wife I want to make it fast, and she hit the roof. "The reception can wait. Don't you say a word about making this a short service." So I say to the priest, "Father, could you make it a short service? Don't say anything to anybody, but I gotta get to work." And I give him a fifty. He starts the service, and it's the slowest service in the history of baptism. I'm looking at my watch, and I'm staring at him, and he's looking at me. And finally, at about 2:30, he suddenly stops and says, "So, Steve—how'm I doing on time?" My wife almost killed me!

I probably should have given him $100 instead of $50.

In my experience, there is no one who can't be tipped. It always works. No one is offended, if you do it

Even more things a goomba would never say:

- What are you lookin' at? Oh, I'm sorry, I thought you were looking in my direction, please excuse me.
- Call my mother what you want. I still say she's a nice lady.
- My fiancée wants a small wedding.
- Could we have a booth over by the window, please?
- Son, I think you'd better take a time out before I really get mad.

right. If they can give you what you want, they'll give you what you want.

Unless they just can't, and all the tipping in the world won't help you then. One pal of mine used to be the captain at the Hilton when Elvis played there in the 1970s. He told me that he'd get lots of extremely rich Japanese customers coming to the show. They'd stand in line and wait to be seated, just like everyone else. Then they'd get up to where he was standing, and they'd see the front row was empty, and they'd start pointing.

Now, the front row, for a big show like Elvis, is always reserved for "comps." These might be high-rollers, or Elvis' mom, or whatever. But you cannot give them to the regular customers standing in line. Not for any kind of a tip. Can't be done.

But these Japanese customers didn't speak much English, so they didn't understand that.

As soon as he would tell them, "No. I can't give you that seat," out would come a hundred dollar bill. And he'd say, "No. I'm sorry. Those are the comp seats. Those are reserved," and out would come *another* hundred dollar bill. So he'd say again, very patiently, "I'm sorry. I can't," and here comes *another* hundred dollar bill. He's making several hundred dollars, per customer, for seats that he can't give away to his best friend.

So you can't get what's not available, no matter how much you tip.

But you'd be surprised how well it can work, even in unexpected places.

Here's a personal story.

I love my mother. She's a wonderful woman. I love her dearly. But like all mothers she can be a little . . . difficult. For years, whenever I go to visit her, it's nothing but complaints. She hates living in Jersey. She misses her life in Brooklyn. The food here is no good. There's no good bakery. The people are terrible. She goes on and on and on! And I gotta listen to it! I don't know what to tell her. What can I do? But before I leave, I always give her a coupla hunge. I say, "Here, take this," and I put $200 in her hand. And she says, "Oh no, you shouldn't, you gave me a hundred last time . . ." But she takes it. And she calms down. After that, everything's nice. So I leave on a nice note.

This goes on for years. Always the same pattern. My mother complains and complains, I give her some money, she stops complaining, and I leave. I finally realize, I'm doing this whole thing backwards!

So I tell my wife, "I can't take this anymore, with the constant complaining. I'm going to give her the money *up front*, and see if that makes her happy."

So the next time I visit, I walk right in the door and

say, "Here's something for you." I give her two brand-new one-hundred-dollar bills. She says, "Oh no, you shouldn't, you gave me a hundred last time . . ." But she takes it.

All of a sudden, there's no complaining! Instead she's treating me extra nice. Can she get me a sandwich? Can she get me a beer? How's the family? It's like I'm the best customer she ever had!

See, she thinks maybe there's some more money coming if I have a good visit. So she's in a good mood, and I'm getting great service!

I told my wife later, "I finally figured my mother out. She's a maitre d'."

On the way out, I pull out another two hundred. She says, "No, please, you shouldn't, you've done enough—" and then, without missing a beat, she sees that it's two one-hundred-dollar bills, again. And she says, "Can you break one of these?"

Never underestimate the power of the tip. Properly applied, it is a wonderful tool.

GOOMBA INSULTS

I KNOW A LOT of people who think a waiter or a maitre d' will be offended or insulted if you try to tip them.

I've never experienced that. They get insulted if you don't tip 'em, or if you're demanding and pushy and you haven't tipped 'em, or if you haven't tipped 'em enough. Most of the time, they appreciate the attention and the money.

But the average goomba can be insulted in other ways. You want to watch out for this. An angry goomba is not a nice goomba. You don't want to make him angry.

It's very easy for one goomba to make fun of another goomba. Guys do it all the time. Look at the nicknames—most of them are ways of poking fun at a guy. You call a guy "Sally Two Times" because he repeats everything he says. You call a guy "Jerry Fingers" because he's a kleptomaniac. Some guys you don't call them the nicknames to their faces because you could get into trouble. No one called Benjamin Siegal "Bugsy" to his face, 'cause he'd go nuts. Tony Spilotro was called "The Ant" because he was so short, but no one called him "The Ant" in person. A guy with a nickname like "Fat Tony," you won't call him that when he's around.

But everyone has a nickname just the same. I don't know for sure why this is. It's not true in other cultures. The Irish don't all call each other Connor "The Nose" Fitzpatrick. The Jews don't call each other Hyman "Two

Guys from the neighborhood hanging out.

Left Feet" Berkowitz. There's all those black blues singers with names like Jefferson "Blind Melon" Washington. But the average African-American doesn't have a nickname alias that everyone calls him unless he's a rapper. Mostly, if his name is Ray, they call him Ray.

Personally, I think the goombas do it because of some traditional mistrust that Italian-Americans had of the law. You use nicknames, instead of last names, so no one who doesn't know who you're talking about will know who you're talking about. Either that, or maybe it's because by the time the goomba is a third-generation American, he can't pronounce the family names anymore. Guys are called things like Ghiglione and Giacomotella—so you call them "Jimmy the Gig" and "Jacky Two Pants" instead.

When I was a kid I knew a guy named Violent Joey. I never knew his last name. When I worked as a maitre d' in Las Vegas, I knew a guy named Tony Bags. His last name was something like "Bagnoli." There was another guy named Pete Cigars. I never knew his last name, but he sure liked to smoke cigars. Another guy is Jimmy the Beak because he has such a big nose. There was another guy who was called Joey Car Service because he worked for a car service. My friend Mike, we call him Mikie Razor Head, because he shaves his head. Mike Razor.

But it gets a little ridiculous. I used to eat in a place that we called Vinny the Zip's. A "zip" is a guy just off the boat. There were two guys who were in Vinny the Zip's joint all the time. One guy was called Vinny the Bear, because he was a huge guy. The other guy was called Skinny Vinny. Some nights Skinny Vinny and Vinny the Bear would both be at Vinny the Zip's at the same time. Thank God there was only three of them.

And nothing's off-limits. I knew a guy named Phil. He had a stroke. After that, he was "Philly the Stroke." There was a guy named Johnny, who had a heart attack. After that, he was always "Johnny Heart Attack." The guy that ran the candy store on my street had lost part of one arm, from the elbow down. His name was "Jimmy One Arm." It wasn't mean. It was just how you identified guys, and how you told the difference between Jimmy One Arm and Jimmy the Gimp. Or whatever.

Same thing with a guy I knew named Nicky the Nap. He's narcoleptic and he falls asleep during dinner!

But you have to be careful. You call a goomba a greaseball, or a wop, you'd better be pretty good friends and you'd better be smiling when you say it. A friend of mine was on an airplane recently and the guy next to him started talking. They were both from New York. My friend, he lives on Staten Island. The other guy goes to Staten Island pretty often. He says, "Once a week, I drive over that guinea gangplank."

My friend almost strangled the guy, because he wasn't Italian.

If you call a guy a "wonder bread wop," you'd better be pretty fast on your feet, or fast with your fists. You can call a guy a "zip," if he's right off the boat from Italy and speaks in broken English. But you'd better be ready for trouble if you say it to the wrong guy.

Some stuff, you can't say at all. You never, never, never make fun of a guy's wife, or daughter, or mother. That's sacred. It's forbidden to speak of it. All that stuff that black guys do—"Yo' Momma so ugly . . ."— goombas don't do that. Can't do that. Guys would kill you for that stuff.

There are some things that you can't joke about even if you're talking to a close friend. Some things are never joked about.

For example: I had a friend named Rocco. His son was Rocco Junior. Nicest people in the world. Very traditional, very Italian. So traditional that when I went to their house for dinner, the mother didn't even sit at the table with us. She only cooked and served. That was the tradition in their house. Very old-world.

So Rocco and his family go on a weekend outing to the Catskills. To the Villa Roma, which was the big Italian resort in the Catskills. They go with some other families. Very nice. At night they go to the dining room where there's a nice Italian singer. They have a nice big Italian meal, then there's a nice Italian comic. He's very funny until he starts doing his "Italian" material. "Why do Italian men grow moustaches?" he asks. "Because they want to look like their mothers." Now, to Rocco, this is not funny. You don't make fun of mothers! But the comic goes on. Now Rocco is really getting upset. He knows it's all a joke, but still! Then the comic says, "What do you call five Italian women in a hot tub? The Bay of Pigs."

Rocco goes nuts. He rushes the stage, screaming in Italian, and almost kills the guy. They have to restrain him. The comic is so terrified that the show can't go on. He can't get back on stage. He refuses to come out. The show is over.

That's very goomba. You don't make fun of mothers. Or women.

Here's another list of words never spoken by a true goomba:

I can't believe I'm a *Jeopardy* champion!
Am I wearing too much jewelry?
Could you give me the telephone number for the nearest Domino's?
I'm late for my Step-Aerobics class.
My uncle Rocco has beautiful hands.
No, my dad never hit me when I was a kid.
Of course I support handgun control legislation.
Why, yes, your honor. I remember *exactly* where I was on the night of June 28.

GOOMBA HOSPITALITY

THE GOOMBA isn't necessarily known for his hospitality. He's not famous for it, the way a Southerner is. It isn't that he's not generous—because he is—but because he doesn't have that tradition of welcoming strangers into his house. The goomba is friendly, but he's more guarded. If he has someone to the house, that's a pretty big deal. This is only for family and very close friends.

Goomba generosity, on the other hand, can get

almost ridiculous. I remember once, when I was in my early twenties, I took a roadtrip through the South. I had decided to move to Vegas 'cause there wasn't anything happening for me at home. I was just going to hit the road with a friend and we decided to drive through New Orleans, just to see it. We filled the car up with supplies—pepperonis, cheeses, all that stuff—and off we went.

Right before we left, my friend Arnold from Brooklyn said, "You're going to New Orleans? Go see Louie, at Louie's Palace. It's right in the middle of the Quarter, off Bourbon Street. Tell him I said 'hello.'"

So, when we got to New Orleans, we went straight to the Quarter, and we found this bar called Louie's Palace. It's late on a Sunday afternoon, in the middle of July. Hot? Ridiculous. Inside, no one's there except this old lady bartender, and one even older guy sitting at the bar drinking.

We say, "Is Louie around?"

The old lady bartender says, "No. Louie's not here."

It's hot, so we decide to have a beer. After a while, I go out to the car and come back with three pepperonis. I say to the old lady bartender, "Would you give these to Louie? We're from Brooklyn, and we're friends of Arnold's, and we just stopped by to say hello."

It turns out the old guy at the bar *is* Louie. And he welcomes us like long lost nephews. He's this ancient wise guy and he's related to one of the biggest mob guys in New Orleans. He'd been a big guy in Brooklyn, but he'd had to leave, like twenty-five years before. And now he's treating two goombas from Brooklyn like they're a couple of celebrities.

For three days it's nonstop, red carpet treatment. Louie wines us and dines us. He takes us to every fancy restaurant in New Orleans. We eat like kings. We go to the track. We go out on a boat. Everything is taken care of, like having the key to the city. One afternoon, we're in this joint, and Louie says, "You wanna get laid?" There's no one around but us and the waitress. I say, "Sure." Next thing I know, I'm upstairs in a little apartment with the waitress.

After three days of this, we left for Las Vegas. We thanked Louie and said we'd see him again someday.

Here's the funny part. It turns out that Louie doesn't know anybody named Arnold from Brooklyn. He doesn't have any idea who that is, or who we are. He left so long ago, and he's so old, that he's forgotten.

All he knows is, here's two guys coming to visit, and they brought three pepperonis.

That's real goomba hospitality, and a real good tip on goomba etiquette: When you go visit someone, you take something. If someone comes to visit, you take care of them.

Chapter 5

GOOMBA HEROES

If you're a guy like me
and you come from
where I come from,
Frank Sinatra is like a god.
Huge. The greatest.
The Chairman.
Like, there's
nobody else like him.

Every culture has its own heroes. Goomba culture is no different. But the goomba role models are not who you think. Just like everyone else, it's world leaders, and athletes, and entertainers your goomba looks up to. It's Joe DiMaggio and Frank Sinatra. And why not? These guys are everybody's heroes; they just happen to be great goombas besides.

The goomba is a modern phenomenon. The real goomba did not even begin to exist until around the end of the nineteenth century, when lots of Italians came to America and started settling in the big cities. That's when there were Italian-Americans, and that's when a certain kind of Italian-American started turning into a goomba.

But way before that, there were people who could

have been goombas if only the idea had been invented. History is littered with great Italians who had the goomba attitude. Some of them did great goomba things and became famous—mostly because they did something important in a very goomba way.

Christopher Columbus. What a great goomba! He wouldn't listen to anyone. He says to the world, "Whadda you mean the world is flat? *Va fangoo!* I'm going to India!" And off he goes. Never mind that he wound up in the New World. He could've done the whole thing singing "My Way." He knew there was something out there, and he decided to go and find it, and he did—with a little help from another great goomba, Amerigo Vespucci, his navigator. Columbus, a native of Genoa, didn't know where he was going, and he didn't know where he was when he got there. But his pal Vespucci put the whole thing together, and that's why they named the country after him. I'm just grateful that they chose his first name and not his last when they decided what to call the country. "Vespu-uci, Vespu-uci, God shed his grace on thee . . ." Fuhgeddaboutit.

Then you've got Dante Alighieri, or just plain Dante: What a scribbler! The greatest! And one of the oldest. The English are just stringing together two or three sentences in the thirteenth century. Chaucer is stumbling along, trying to write one paragraph that makes sense. And look at this goomba! He falls in love with a chick named Beatrice, and then writes *The Divine Comedy* for her—in 1315! It's still one of the three or four most important pieces of world literature. And *The Inferno*? Purgatory! Paradise! If I was ever going to read a single book, this would *definitely* be it.

Marco Polo: The bold adventurer! This guy goes to China, for some reason, and brings back pasta, chopsticks, and gunpowder. What, no egg rolls? Italians have been going out for Chinese ever since.

Galileo: Even more than Columbus, what balls on the guy! The Pope wants to burn him at the stake because he insists that the earth moves around the sun, not the other way around—and he tells the Pope to take a hike. The Inquisition is on. They're gonna kill the guy. And he still insists the earth goes around the sun. What nerve! An Italian, telling the Pope to piss off. What a goomba!

Leonardo da Vinci: Inventor of the reflecting telescope and the helicopter. Sculptor. Painter. Genius! Goomba? Don't think so.

Michelangelo: Like Leonardo, what a genius! Look at the ceiling of the Sistine Chapel in the Vatican. Look at his *Pietà*. Now look at *The Last Supper*. The guy had food on his mind, like every good goomba.

Guiseppe Verdi: *Il Trovatore. La Traviata. Aida!* What an entertainer. He's got guys in tights prancing around the stage, singing songs in Italian. And he's not a fruit! Imagine what a set of barbells this guy had to have. It's 1860. The other Italians are fighting wars of unification and he's writing opera. That's class.

Benito Mussolini: Nah. Forget him. Fascist asshole.

More modern goombas have contributed heavily to the worlds of art and commerce. There's Fellini, with the movies, and Ferrari, with the race cars. And Lamborghini. And Rossellini. And the parents of Sophia Loren and Anna Magnani and other Italian beauties of the cinema.

And then there's Frank. Francis Albert Sinatra. The Chairman of the Board.

If you're a guy like me and you come from where I come from, Frank Sinatra is like a god. Huge. The greatest. The Chairman. Like, there's nobody else like him. I am a huge Sinatra fan. No one impresses me— but this guy impressed me. One of the biggest thrills of my whole life was having dinner with Frank. Except it wasn't like you'd expect.

I was friends with Jilly's son—Jilly Rizzo, who was the owner of the famous Jilly's in New York, where Frank hung out, and who became Frank's best friend. They went everywhere together. You never saw Frank

Jilly's seventieth birthday, Vegas.

without Jilly. And I was living with Jilly's son. At that time I was a maitre d' at The Riviera. And Frank was in town, playing at Bally's. And I got the call: You're invited to this thing, for dinner, with Frank. It's Jilly Rizzo's seventieth birthday party. At two o'clock in the morning, at the Italian restaurant at The Riviera.

I don't know why we were meeting at The Riv, because Sinatra always ate at a place called Villa D'Este. Later it was changed to Pierro's. All the mobsters in Vegas ate there. But tonight it was The Riv.

A few years later, when he played The Riv, the management built a suite to Frank's specifications. It was on the twenty-ninth floor there, a two-bedroom suite the hotel had built special for him.

There's like twenty-five people there when I arrive. Everyone's sitting at this huge L-shaped table. Sinatra's there already, wearing this sort of record company jacket with his name stitched onto the left breast—like anybody's not gonna know who he is! Jilly's wearing this matching jacket, with his name on it, too. All around them, there's Sinatra's wife, Barbara, and these local comics like Jerry Vale, and Bernie Allen, and Don Rickles.

Rickles is on—like, he's never *not* on, but tonight he's really on. He's killing everybody. He says to Jerry Vale, "Look around, Jerry. Doesn't this feel like you're in show business? Doesn't this feel almost like you're finally in show business?" Jerry Vale, who's been playing Vegas for, like, three hundred years.

The only problem is, Sinatra's drunk. He was drunk when he got there, and now he's got a bottle of Jack Daniel's in front of him, and now he's really drunk. Everyone is eating. It's something like three o'clock in the morning now. We're eating provolone, and salami, and mozzarella, and then there's big plates of pasta and osso bucco.

It's always tense when Sinatra's around, incredibly tense, even when it's just friends. Everything has to be just right. The Jack has to be on the table when he arrives. The ice cubes have to be special—he had to have round ones, instead of square ones, or something like that. This night was just like that. Everyone was very tense.

Except Rickles. This guy's going nuts. Everybody's laughing.

But not Frank. He's not laughing. After a while, he starts to say some nice stuff about Jilly. He raises his glass, and he says, "To the best friend I've ever had in the whole world," and people clap and everything, and then Jilly gets up to make a speech. And Rickles is still talking. He never stops talking. Jilly's making the speech, and Rickles is, like, talking *over* him.

Sinatra starts screaming, "Let him talk, Don. Shut your mouth. Shut your goddam mouth!"

Rickles laughed. No one got mad. This is just the way they all talked to each other. They were all very good friends.

I had a long talk later with Jilly. He told me about being in Lake Tahoe with Sinatra, when Sinatra was going out with Marilyn Monroe. She was up in Tahoe with him, and she'd had too much to drink. She's passed out, from the booze and the pills and whatever else she was on. She's sleeping on a sofa, wrapped up in this blanket. Frank says, "Get her out of here, Jilly. Take her into the other room."

So Jilly picks her up in his arms and takes her into

the other room. Now the blanket is falling off her. She's completely naked. Jilly puts her down on the bed, and he just stares at her. She has the most perfect body anyone has ever seen. Jilly can't believe it. But he can't do anything about it! On the other hand, no one's looking. So he leans over and takes a big lick of her left tit. And then covers her up real quick.

The last time I saw Jilly was about five years later—at his funeral, down in Palm Springs. We buried Jilly, and then there was a party back at Sinatra's place. Everyone's standing around. It's pretty sad, you know. Lots of Vegas people are there: Paul Anka, Roger Moore, other Hollywood people. There were pictures all over the house of Frank with these people—Frank and JFK, Frank and Bobby Kennedy, Frank and Ella Fitzgerald . . . Everyone's drinking and sad.

And Barbara Sinatra comes up to me, out of nowhere, and says, "Have you had a chance to try the jalapeño pie? It's fabulous." Jalapeño pie! Her husband's best friend in the world has just died, and she's talking about the jalapeño pie! I don't know why I remember it, but that's what she said. Jalapeño pie.

A friend of mine, a great old-time Vegas guy, told me a wonderful story about Sinatra and Tony Bennett. Frank was sailing on a yacht somewhere out in the Azores Islands. He's got about twenty of his favorite people on the boat with him. And he tells them, "I'm gonna get you something for dinner that'll knock your socks off." Then he calls this friend of his at The Sands in Vegas. He knows Tony Bennett is playing that night. And he gets the friend to go to the sound man, who's running Tony's show, and gets *him* to run a speaker wire from Tony's show right into the telephone lines. Frank has his people on the boat hook the telephone up to a set of speakers. And right during dinner, he makes this announcement to the people on the boat: "You're about to hear the greatest singer in the world." He turns the speakers on, and his guests have got Tony Bennett serenading them, live, from Las Vegas and The Sands hotel.

Now, that's goomba living! Even if you're not Italian, don't you want to live like that? This is what heroes are made of—especially goomba heroes.

HOLLYWOOD GOOMBAS

HOLLYWOOD HAS HAD a love affair with the goomba world since the early days of the movies. There are dozens of great goomba movies. Some of them are sort of pro-goomba, and some of them are sort of anti-goomba. But they paint the picture of real goomba life.

And most self-respecting goombas have copies of some or all these pictures on their video and DVD racks. Here's a sample of movies you must see if you want to understand the goomba—or be one!

> *The Godfather* (all three parts, but especially I and II)
> *GoodFellas*
> *Mean Streets*
> *Casino*
> *Carlito's Way*
> *Scarface*
> *Donnie Brasco*
> *The Untouchables*

You notice right off that those movies have a few things in common. First, they're all made by Italians and they star Italians—Coppola, De Niro, Scorsese, Pacino, De Palma . . . You get the picture. But there's plenty of other movies made by other guys, or starring other guys, that are also a good look at goomba life.

> *Moonstruck*
> *Saturday Night Fever*
> *The Pope of Greenwich Village*
> *Miller's Crossing*
> *Heat*

On the Waterfront
Once Upon a Time in America
The Sicilian
Reservoir Dogs

There's also quite a few movies that have some fun with the goomba thing. They're not mean-spirited. They . . . *amuse* me.

Analyze This
Mickey Blue Eyes
My Cousin Vinny

And lastly there is one movie that really doesn't have anything to do with the goomba thing, but represents the things that goombas believe in. Every goomba has to have a copy. And watch it routinely.

Rocky.

That's it. Everything else is optional.

There are also lots of great moments in Hollywood movies that could become goomba moments if someone wrote the dialogue different. If goombas ran Hollywood, all the great lines from all the great movies would have to be changed to goomba lines.

"Frankly, my dear, I don't give a fuck."

"ET, phone home—and wire me twenty large."

"Go ahead, make my day—tell me the Giants covered."

"There's no place like Scores, there's no place like
   Scores . . ."

"I coulda been somebody. I coulda been a contender.
   Instead of what I am today. Which is a cooperating
   witness in the relocation program . . ."

Of course now some people might consider me a Hollywood goomba since I've kind of made a career from playing them on TV and in the movies.

It wasn't overnight. I did my first audition for the movie *Indecent Proposal* in 1993. I didn't get the job. I didn't go up for another job for a couple of years. Then I got the part in *Casino* in 1995. Then I got a part in *Fear and Loathing in Las Vegas,* with Johnny Depp and Benecio Del Toro. I played a bouncer in a Vegas nightclub. I wrestle around with Benecio and throw him to the ground. I broke my watch doing that scene—which, incidentally, we didn't shoot in Vegas. We were supposed to, but they ran over and didn't have time. A month later they flew me to Los Angeles and we shot the scene at the old Ambassador Hotel, where Bobby Kennedy was killed.

Then I did a movie with Joe Mantegna and Courteney

Cox, called *The Runner*. We shot it in Wendover, Nevada, the armpit of the world. I played a pit boss. After that, I got a job on *Chicago Hope,* and a part in a movie called *Detroit Rock City,* about the band KISS.

And that's where something changed. I had this big scene, with Kevin Corrigan and Natasha Lyonne. I was in Toronto. I did the scene with these two really respected actors, and I hung in there. For the first time I realized I could hold my own with the pros. I called my wife and said, "I know I can do this thing."

Three months later I got an agent, and I started taking acting classes.

See, I did the whole thing in reverse. I got the jobs, then I got the agent, and *then* I started trying to figure out what the hell I was doing.

I think that's part of why I got the jobs, though. I had a day job. I had a family. I was not some starving, struggling actor who's gonna die if he doesn't get the part. I had some confidence.

Plus I worked hard at it. I did what needed to be done. There were some days where I'd show up for work at noon—and I had already flown to LA, and back, to do an audition. On my own time, on my own dime, because I wanted it. Some guys would say, "They're not flying me down there? Fuck 'em." Not me. If I wanted the part, I did what needed to be done.

Another big break for me was *The Flintstones: Viva Rock Vegas*. But I almost screwed that one up. See, I never saw the first Flintstones movie. I went in to read for the director, Brian Levant. The part was for this mob guy. So I read it like a mob guy. I said stuff like, "Get the money, Rocco, or we'll kill you." I was menacing, you know? Turns out, I was too menacing. After the audition, the casting guy said, "Jesus, Steve. This is a kids' movie. You'll scare them right out of the theater." They asked me to do the part more "cartoony," and I couldn't. I didn't know how. So I didn't get the part. I got a smaller part instead.

Again, another guy would have said, "I didn't get the big part. Fuck 'em." Not me. If I couldn't get the big part, I was happy to get the small part. I got a lot of parts that way.

I got the *Sopranos* gig by accident—which is the way all the best things in life happen. A friend of mine was getting married in New York. So I went out from Las Vegas for the wedding. I called my agent, first, and said, "See if you can get me to read for that new show on HBO, *The Sopranos*." So I get a shot to go in and audition. They've got me up for the part of this FBI agent. I read, and the casting director says, "I don't see you as an FBI guy. But maybe I can see you as this other guy, this Bacala guy." So I read for that, and they say they'll call me. A while later they do call me. They say, "Can you come in and read for David Chase—the executive producer?" But by now I'm back in Vegas. And they're not offering to fly me back. It's on my dime. I told my wife, "I'm don't want to spend the money. I probably won't get the part anyway." She said, "Go. Go take a shot. What have you got to lose? Go." So I went. I got the gig. If it hadn't been for that wedding, I wouldn't have read for the show. And if it hadn't been for my wife, I wouldn't have flown back there on my own dime, to read the second time. My whole life, today, would be different. All thanks to my wife, Laura.

It's been a real challenge. Some parts more than others. I love it, and I love the cast and the crew. It's like

Michael Imperioli, Joe Pantiliano, and Tony Sirico.

My good friend Dominic Chianese. Second season premier.

a big family—a big Italian family. It's really tight, and it's really tight-lipped. Like, I could tell you what it's really like, but someone would probably get whacked. I could tell you who gets whacked at the end of the season, but then it would probably end up being me.

My most famous scene, so far, is probably the scene where we're all out in the woods in the wintertime. In the show, I get this call in the middle of the night, and I have to go up there. I show up wearing all this ridiculous winter clothing. And the scene calls for Tony Soprano to laugh really hard when he sees me the first time.

Now, Jimmy—that's James Gandolfini, who plays Tony Soprano—has seen me, in wardrobe and all, wearing all this stuff. So, how am I going to get that big laugh? I asked the prop guy if he's got anything I can use to make the outfit look more ridiculous. We look through his prop kit and get some stuff.

The actual shot you saw, that's me, in the winter clothes, with this enormous two-foot-long dildo sticking out of my pants. That part's not in the shot, but that's what I was wearing when Jimmy saw me. That's what got the huge laugh. After that, for some other takes, I wore a bras-siere and panties over my

James Gandolfini and me, as Santa. Third season.

winter clothes, and in another one I was wearing this rasta wig. But the dildo got the laugh.

Even after I got the *Sopranos* gig, which is the dream job of all time, I didn't stop with that. And the parts kept coming. Again, some guys would've said, "I'm there. I made it." Not me. I saw this as a great opportunity to continue working. So I keep working.

I got a big part in this movie *See Spot Run,* with David Arquette and Paul Sorvino. I was supposed to play the part of this not-too-smart wise guy. Me and another guy have to chase down this dog. I went in to read for the director and the producers and about five other people. Halfway through, the producer jumps up and says, "You're the guy! You're the guy!" That had never happened to me before. The movie turned out good. At least I didn't scare the kids out of the theater.

The auditions don't always go that way. I went in to read for a part that called for a "Bavarian" accent. It was for a big Bavarian bookmaker, with a Bavarian accent. Bavarian? I didn't even know what that was. I went in, and I said, "I don't know how to do this." They said, "Don't worry. Just be yourself." So I was. It didn't work out. I don't sound "Bavarian." Whatever that is. I told the casting director, "See? I told you."

Sometimes I would go on auditions and I would run into comics that I had booked into the comedy club at The Riviera. They'd always act surprised—and a little condescending. Like it was cute that I was going for the part, or something. They'd say, "What are *you* doing here?" I was, like, "What the hell do you *think* I'm doing here? Same as you." They'd say, "I didn't know you were an actor." Then I started booking some jobs. I started getting more parts than some of these guys were getting. One day I went into an audition and there was a couple of these guys there. I said, "One guy asks me what I'm doing here, I swear I'm gonna slap him." Nobody asked.

Overall, I get a lot more parts than I lose. And I think the whole goomba attitude has a lot to do with it. When an actor goes in for a part he really wants, the casting director can smell the desperation. And it's not attractive. It makes you seem weak or something. Me, I never *had* to have the part. I wanted the part. But I wasn't going to die, or starve, if I didn't get it. It was more like a hobby with me, at the beginning. So, I kind of didn't care.

Now that it's in my blood, I care about it more than anything else. With the exception of my family, that's *all* I care about.

But in the early days, maybe that made it seem like I had the balls for the part, even if I didn't have the resume. I never went into the room intimidated. Some guys feel intimidated, and they freak out and they freeze.

Me, I been in lots of tough spots. Much tougher spots than an audition with some producers from Hollywood. There's no pressure there. You want pressure? How about eight guys coming after you with a baseball bat? That's pressure!

HONORARY GOOMBAS

NOT EVERY GREAT Italian is a goomba, of course. But then again, some of the world's greatest goombas are not goombas at all. Some of them are not even Italian.

James Caan, who was in *The Godfather,* is Jewish. But I've heard him say he's more Italian than most of the

Italians he knows. He's a tough guy. He's a sort of Jewish goomba, if there is such a thing. The English actor Bob Hoskins could be a goomba, too, if he wasn't English. He's pretty tough.

But Mario Cuomo, a fine man and a fine Italian-American, is not a goomba. Rudy Giuiliani is not a goomba. (Former senator Alfonse D'Amato, however, probably is.) Martin Scorsese, whose movies *Mean Streets* and *GoodFellas* put the goomba life on the American cultural map, is actually not a goomba. He's too big an intellectual and not physical enough. But Francis Ford Coppola, the guy that made *The Godfather* and its sequels, is definitely a goomba sort of guy. There's the wine, to start with, and the food. This guy likes to live!

Some people qualify as goomba heroes just because of the way they are. They live like goombas. They got goomba-sized appetites and personalities. If they were Italian, it would be automatic. Here are some examples:

Elvis Presley

Arnold Schwarzenegger

Rosie O'Donnell

Sinbad

Milton Berle (May he rest)

Buddy Hackett

Paul Rodriguez

Still more things a goomba would never say:

- My favorite band ever? The Grateful Dead.
- Let's rent *Godfather III* again.
- Robert De Niro . . . now what was he in again?
- Frank and Tony were good but they weren't a pimple on Perry Como's ass.
- Vince Lombardi was a jerk.

There are also people who could never, never be a goomba, no matter how hard they try, no matter how much they may pretend. Some of them are just genetically wrong for goomba—anyone from the Bush or Kennedy families, for example. You want a goomba president, look for somebody like Teddy Roosevelt, or Bill Clinton.

There's several reasons you'll probably never see a goomba president. Here are a few:

There's no off-track betting offices in D.C.

Big Pussy is an inappropriate Secret Service code name for the president.

His bullet-proof vest would become entangled in thick body hair.

Soft money donations won't fit in plain paper bags.

The impeachment process has no relocation program.

Sit-down with world leaders required before Saddam
    assassination can be ordered.

Tabloid reporters would have to learn to spell "goomar."

The president would look undignified rolling out the first
    bocci ball.

Too expensive to cover all White House furniture in plastic.

Cement truck would look out of place parked in front of
    the White House.

The president can't wear a sweat suit while delivering the
    State of the Union address.

Some other people might be goombas, but they could
never show it. The Pope might be a goomba, for example, but who would ever know?

You also meet people who are pretending to be
goombas. They're like goomba wanna-be's. Some of
these are actors, trying to appear to be goombas in
movies or in TV shows. Maybe it's Billy Crystal, doing
his work opposite a real goomba like Robert De Niro,
in *Analyze This*. Maybe it's Hugh Grant, opposite James
Caan, in *Mickey Blue Eyes*. Remember that? The poor
guy couldn't even say "fuhgeddaboudit." Every time he
tried, he sounded like *Goodbye Mr. Chips*. In both cases

the comedy comes from the soft guy trying to sound like a hard guy.

Some of these pretend goombas are just tough guys, or wanna-be tough guys—cab drivers or waiters or blackjack dealers or football coaches or whatever. They take their tips from the movies, too. They say things like, "You talkin' to me?" like in that scene from *Taxi Driver*. Or they say things like, "You want a piece of me?" Don't let guys like that worry you too much. They'd fold like a Taliban tent if a real goomba confronted them.

GAY GOOMBAS

WHAT ARE YOU, kidding? Fuhgeddaboudit. That ain't funny.

GOOMBA SPORTS HEROES

MOST PEOPLE don't think of professional sports when they think goomba. Or, if they do, they think of it the wrong way: Al Capone, cracking someone's head open with a baseball bat. But there have been some great goomba athletes. Some of the biggest goomba heroes of all time were sports heroes.

Joe DiMaggio: The greatest of all time. He was a New York Yankee outfielder and one of most beautiful players that ever swung a bat. He was tall and handsome, and he was the American League MVP, and he was boning Marilyn Monroe! Later, he became Mr. Coffee, and made a bag of money on television. An all-around hero.

Yogi Berra: Another Yankee legend, Yogi was also a three-time American League MVP, and he played in the World Series fourteen times. What a guy! He's probably most famous for saying, "It ain't over till it's over." No one really knows what this means. But it's pure goomba.

Phil Rizzuto: Another great Yankee player, back in the day. He was a record-breaking shortstop and the fastest guy on the field. Later, he became a television pitchman for an outfit called The Money Store. That was a non-goomba job, but, hey, you do what you gotta do. Yogi Berra thought that getting away from Rizzuto was a good reason for Joltin' Joe to marry Marilyn. He said, about the marriage, "I don't know if it's good for baseball, but it sure beats the hell out of rooming with Phil Rizzuto."

Non-Italians didn't think much of Rizzuto's chances of making it as a pro ballplayer. Casey Stengel, manager of the Brooklyn Dodgers, turned him down after a Dodger try-out, and said to him, "Kid, you're too small. You ought to go out and shine shoes." Phil had one of his best years in professional ball in 1949— the year the Yankees named Stengel their manager.

Leo Durocher: The great goomba baseball manager. He was a legendary tough guy, and took no nonsense from his players or anybody else. He took his teams to the pennant race, and won, three times. He's famous for saying, "Nice guys finish last." He could also have said, "Wise guys finish first." But he didn't.

Rocky Marciano: The greatest goomba boxer of all time. He was world heavyweight champ from 1952 to 1956, and he retired undefeated. He was a feature on the New York nightclub circuit, and a dapper gentleman, despite the fact that he ran around with guys who were connected.

Rocky Graziano: Not the most important Rocky, but a champ just the same. He wore the middleweight belt in 1947 and 1948.

Jake LaMotta: Another great champ. He took the middleweight belt for the years 1949 to 1951, and was the subject of that great Italian-American director Martin Scorsese's movie *Raging Bull,* starring that great goomba actor Robert De Niro.

Vince Lombardi: Green Bay, Wisconsin, ain't exactly prime goomba geography, but this great goomba football coach took his Packers to five National League championships and won two Super Bowl victories. He was legendarily tough, and if he were around today he'd probably kick your ass. He'd be in his nineties, but he'd probably still kick your ass.

For some reason, goombas don't excel in certain sports. We don't produce a lot of great basketball players or hockey players. You almost never hear about a great goomba polo player. Or water polo player. Or championship water skier. Or snow skier, for that matter. Or surfer. Your average goomba doesn't like to get too cold or too wet. Your average goomba doesn't like

Can you pick out the goomba here? John Jay College, 1976.

the outdoors. You take a goomba far from the city, he's hurting. He needs concrete, and traffic, and takeout Chinese food. Plus he likes to stay out late, drinking and smoking and chasing women. This is not proper training for most professional sports. Only in baseball and boxing can you train in this manner.

Some sports are just not possible for the goomba. He can play a pretty good game of pool, but he's not going to be any good at archery. He can probably drive a Javelin, but he ain't gonna throw the javelin. He can hold his own in a fight, but he's not gonna look too good in one of those g-strings doing the Greco-Roman take-downs. Golf? No. Tennis? No. Volleyball? Come on. Your goomba is going to hunt a little, and maybe fish a little. He may know how to box, or work the speed bag and the heavy bag. But that's about it. He's got the sweat suit. He just doesn't like to sweat.

THE GOOMBA GANGSTER

IF WE DON'T say it here, someone else will point it out. So, what the hell? There's lots of notable goombas who got famous for being wise guys. Everybody in the world has heard about Al Capone and Lucky Luciano. Everybody knows about John Gotti. People know names like Gambino, or Genevose, Colombo, Giancana, Bonanno, or Luchese. Sometimes the familiarity with these names eclipses other facts about Italian-American life. Everyone knows Al Capone was Italian. Most people don't think of Joe DiMaggio as anything but a great ball player. (It's part of American history, and it's too bad. Say "Abbot and Costello," and everyone knows you're talking about comedy and "Who's on first?" and all that. Say "Lou Costello," and people will automatically think "gangster.") People think they know about La Cosa Nostra, or The Black Hand. They think they know about Sicily.

Worse, they think this gangster stuff means Italian, or goomba. It doesn't. Knowing the difference could keep you out of some serious trouble. So, know the difference.

Just so there's no confusion here, let's get one thing straight: I play a gangster on TV but I'm not a gangster myself. I've never been a gangster. I don't want to be a gangster. My job on *The Sopranos* and in the movies, is just a job. I take it very seriously, but I know the difference between what I am and what I play.

Some people might not know this. I get stopped on the street by people who call me "Bobby" or "Bacala." They seem surprised to discover that I'm not a moron.

It's called *acting*. I was always a goomba, but I became a notable goomba because of acting.

Chapter 6

GOOMBA FOOD

You never eat salami

with mayonnaise.

Never.

This is a sin.

Anyone who's been around Italians knows that food is the center of everything. This is quadruple true of the goomba. Family is the glue that holds goomba culture together. Food is the glue that holds the family together. The evening meal, the Sunday supper, the shopping and the cooking, the dining and the discussions about dining . . . Food rules the goomba world.

If you saw *The Godfather*, or *GoodFellas*, you know.

Remember? In *The Godfather*, there is a series of scenes that takes place when Michael Corleone is getting ready to go to the big sit-down with the men who murdered his father. They think he's coming to make peace. He's actually coming to kill them. He's never done anything like this before—until now, he's been kept away from the family business. He's nervous, and he's scared, and he's being kept hidden in a secret apartment, guarded by all the loyal Corleone foot soldiers.

And what are the foot soldiers doing? They're cooking tomato sauce. To calm Michael down, one of them explains very gently how the sauce must be cooked.

Remember *GoodFellas*? There's two scenes that stand out. First of all is when our hero Henry Hill gets sent to prison, along with his godfather, played by Paul Sorvino, and a bunch of the other *capos* from their outfit. They're in prison. What are they doing? They're cooking tomato sauce! One guy is in charge of slicing garlic, with a razor blade, so thin it melts in the pot. Another guy is putting away groceries—steaks and chops and loaves of bread and bottles of wine. In prison!

Later, when the world is falling down around his head, when the Feds are onto him, when the family has turned against him and abandoned him, Henry Hill is going nuts. He's addicted to drugs, and he's running drugs and drug runners in and out of Kennedy. He's got cash and cocaine going in and out. He's hiding from helicopters and undercover cops. And what is he doing? He's cooking spaghetti and meatballs! He's got pasta sauce on the stove, and he's driving his drug runner to the airport, and he's telling his little brother not to forget to stir the sauce . . . while he's staring down death, drug addiction, and federal agents!

Some goombas I know, food is all they think about. Food is the main connection they have to their culture. Some of them only can speak Italian when they're talking about food. The only Italian words they know are words for food—'scarole, scungilli, ricotta, calamar'. Without the food, they'd just be *amerigan*—like every other American.

With the food, though, the culture is elevated to an art form. Social gatherings are all built around the food, whether it's a wedding, a funeral, a baptism, a communion, a sit-down—whatever! You gotta eat. And you gotta eat the right food, in the right order, and it's got to be cooked the right way. Many a goomba argument has started over food, and some of these arguments never end. It's worse than politics and sports. Anybody can forgive a friend for voting the wrong way or betting the wrong way. But if a guy doesn't like your mother's cooking—forget it. He's history. He's worse than dead. He's out.

It's a very personal thing, cooking. I know guys who won't eat Italian food cooked by anybody but their wives, anyplace but their home. And when a guy like that invites you to eat with him, you know it's an honor. A guy invites you to his home, it's always an honor, but

Things you'll never hear a goomba say about food:

- Is this low in fat and cholesterol?
- I got a real craving for corned beef and cabbage.
- Could I get a doggy bag for this?
- I think these carrot sticks gave me agita.
- I'd like to order a Juice Man Juicer, please.

if his wife is serving macaroni, that's really special. You eat with extra appetite, and you better like it.

My grandmother was a wonderful cook, a well-known cook, famous for her Italian cooking in a neighborhood full of Italians. She'd cook eggplant parmegiana, and sell it to the local Italian deli, The Emilio Brothers. They'd freeze it and put their own label on it. That's how good it was. Everyone knew it was hers, but everyone bought it at The Emilio Brothers just like it was made by The Emilio Brothers. That was just the way the neighborhood was. People would talk like this.

"You want a good *melanzane,* you go to Emilio Brothers."

"The best! Just like homemade!"

"It *is* homemade. You know who makes it?"

"Don't insult me. I've eaten it in her very house."

"For *melanzane parmigiana,* The Emilio Brothers! That's the best!"

Don't be confused by your ideas about goombas in the kitchen. Cooking Italian is a very masculine thing. I know some very tough guys who like to spend an hour every Sunday in their backyards, tending to their gardens, where they're growing the ingredients for their sauce. They got the tomatoes, and the peppers, and the basil, and oregano. They take it very seriously, and when they get down to the cooking, it's very manly business. Women make great cooks. But a goomba man also has a place in the kitchen.

HOW TO EAT LIKE A GOOMBA

MOST PEOPLE don't know how to eat a proper Italian meal. They don't know how to order it. They don't know what they're *supposed* to order. They're doing it all wrong. This is the classic Italian dinner. This is how you order it. This is how you eat it.

You have to start with a nice antipasto, a nice *cold*

antipasto. It must consist of a big platter, and it has to have some prosciutto, some salami, some fresh mozzarella, some provolone—all of this imported, now—some black olives and some roasted peppers. It has to have some fresh tomatoes. It has to have a loaf of nice Italian bread, with a nice crust, and some good olive oil on the side.

None of this is optional. It's not negotiable. This is mandatory.

Then you have a hot appetizer. Maybe it's a nice fried calamari. Maybe it's a baked clams *oreganato*. Maybe some plates of pasta. Whatever you like. Maybe it's a linguini or a rigatoni, with a marinara sauce, or a vodka sauce, or a Sunday sauce.

I'm not talking nouveau Italian, whatever that is. I'm talking very traditional Italian dinner.

Then for the main item you're going to have a nice veal dish. Maybe it's a veal picatta, or an osso bucco, or a chicken parmigiana, or even an eggplant parmigiana. Maybe it's a nice steak.

While you're eating this, you're gonna be drinking a nice Italian red wine. Maybe a Chianti. Maybe a Ruffino. A heavy red wine with a lot of body. You don't go for the red? Maybe you drink a nice pinot grigio.

After dinner, you're going to finish off with an espresso, and a Sambucca or a little grappa. You're going to have a little cannoli, or a little tiramisu. A nice sweet.

This is the perfect goomba dinner. This is the goomba version of the perfectly balanced diet—cold antipasto, hot antipasto, a big main dish, and a dessert, with plenty of red wine. Beautiful.

Now, you invite Italians for that meal, everyone's gonna be happy. This is the classic goomba dinner. And you can find this meal in every city in America. There is one great Italian restaurant in every city in America. You could eat like this every night, if you knew where to go.

GOOMBA FOOD DO'S AND DON'TS

THERE ARE CERTAIN things you can't do with Italian food. And certain things to watch out for so you don't get into trouble.

You never drink milk with dinner. I don't know why. But if you order a glass of milk with a plate of pasta, you're gonna get smacked. My father would knock me out of my chair if I asked for that at home.

You never ask for grated Parmesan on anything with fish or shellfish in it. I don't know why. Maybe it's the seafood and the dairy? I don't know. Some restaurants, they won't give it to you even if you insist on it.

My dad, 1947.

You never, ever ask for mayonnaise with your antipasto. You never eat salami with mayonnaise. Never. This is a sin.

You can tell the quality of an Italian restaurant by the bread. Look for a nice crisp loaf, with a nice thick crust. If they bring you a limp hunk of bread with no crust, like they serve in a sandwich shop, you might as well get up and walk out now. The food is going to be terrible.

You can tell the quality of a restaurant by the items on the menu, too. If they serve a pizza with pineapple and ham on it, get out at once. No goomba would ever, ever eat a pizza with pineapple on it. Or a pizza with goat cheese and radicchio. Or a pizza with sprouts. This is California crap that no self-respecting goomba would touch.

You probably can't get a decent meal any place that's selling "homemade" pasta, either. Or "fresh" pasta. No goomba makes his own pasta. And most of them don't call it "pasta" in the first place. It's macaroni, or it's linguini, or penne, or spaghetti, or whatever. I don't know when macaroni turned into pasta. But it wasn't a goomba that called it that.

No self-respecting goomba will eat in one of these chain Italian places, either. You will never see a goomba in a Macaroni Grill, or a Buca Di Beppo, or an Olive

Garden. He might make the mistake of going once, but no goomba would ever eat there twice.

And you should never eat in a restaurant that has a sign saying "Authentic Italian." This is a lie. It isn't authentic, or they would never put the sign there.

SOPRANO SUPPERS

ON THE *Sopranos* set, the catering is all Italian food. A lot of the cast and crew is Italian. The caterer cooks mostly Italian. There's fresh pasta and bread and antipasto all day long. Fresh mozzarella. Provolone. Salami. Anytime you get a break, you go and eat.

We shoot in Long Island, in Queens, right under the 59th Street bridge. There are location shoots all over Jersey. This ain't LA. This is a very New York show. And a lot of the guys on the show were raised right around there. There's some Brooklyn guys, and some Jersey guys. James Gandolfini, he's from Jersey. A lot of the guys were born and raised and still live in the neighborhoods where all this action takes place.

Each episode takes about ten days to shoot. It's like a little movie, each time. Not like some sitcom. David Chase is very hands-on with the writing, and the casting, and the music, and the lighting, and everything. That's why it goes so slow, and also why it's one of the greatest shows in the history of television. David Chase is a genius, and this is *his* show. Every part of it is him.

Each week, you get your script for the week. It's very high security. Each script is numbered, and each person has his own personal number. And each script has a note on it that reminds you not to discuss the contents with anyone not employed by Soprano Productions. It's very confidential. And I'm very careful about it. Even my wife doesn't know what's going to happen.

What happens first is, everybody who's in that week's cast—maybe fifty people in all—comes for the table read. Everybody gets together in this big room, around this giant table, for the read-through.

You introduce yourself. You say your name and the name of your character. And then you read. You read the whole thing. From front to back. David and the writers like to hear the words. They might make changes later. The director might talk to you about the scene later. The reading takes about an hour and a half.

And, the good news is, there's always food. Even the table read is catered. There's plenty to eat. So you take a break and have a meal. There's always lots of food,

John Ventimiglia's not a real chef—he just plays one on T.V.

everywhere, with *The Sopranos*. It's like a big Italian family—very professional, but very warm, very supportive. And like any Italian family, they gotta keep everyone happy. So, goomba style, there's lots of food around.

Mostly it's easy to separate the show from real life. But not always. One time a bunch of us went to dinner. When the check came I picked it up. Jimmy—I mean,

James Gandolfini—reached for it, too. But I had it. And he got mad. He got upset. He got *really* upset. He started telling me to give him the check. I said, "Hey! Who do you think you are? Tony Soprano? You're not Tony Soprano—not right now—and I'm not working for you!" He laughed.

The guys on the *Sopranos* get together sometimes to eat afterwards, too. In fact, we have this little tradition. When you die, you get a dinner.

It started with John Fiore. He died—his character died, I mean—in episode number eight. On his last day of work I offered to take him to dinner. Another guy said he'd come too. Then another guy. Pretty soon it was ten or twelve of us, and we all went to dinner at Il Cortile. It's my favorite restaurant in New York—in Little Italy, right on Mulberry Street. We ate and drank and had a big time. And from that day on we decided, whoever gets killed on the show gets a dinner at Il Cortile.

Now, of course, nobody wants a dinner. Nobody wants to get killed on the show. But everyone thinks they're *gonna* get killed on the show. We're always asking each other, "Have you heard anything? Are they gonna kill me? Am I gonna get it? You gotta tell me!" It's just like the real Mafia, because you never know until it's too late. Everyone thinks they might be next, and you're always gonna be the last one to find out.

. . . you gotta eat the right food, in the right order, and it's got to be cooked the right way.

HOW TO COOK LIKE A GOOMBA

THIS CHAPTER is a cooking chapter. It has all the recipes your average goomba is going to need to be a great Italian cook. You can cook more complicated stuff. You can cook simpler stuff. But this is the basics here. This is what you cook for Sunday dinner for you and the friends, or for late night snack for you and your goomar. It's for special occasions and everyday eating, too. It's not supposed to be difficult. Any idiot can do it. If you cook this stuff and it doesn't taste good to you, forget it—you ain't no goomba, pal. Hang it up, or check out the Cordon Bleu. Maybe you're French or something.

So if you want to think like a goomba, you gotta learn to cook like a goomba. Actually, even if you *don't* wanna think like a goomba, this is a great time for you to learn to cook like one. That way, no matter where you are, you can always eat like one.

These are solid Italian recipes.

Tomato Sauce
(aka "Gravy," or Sunday Sauce)

This is the basic recipe for the most basic sauce in Italian cooking. This is the marinara. This is the root. All other recipes grow out from this one. If you can do this, if you can do only this, you can qualify for goomba status in the kitchen. If you can't do this, you are not going to make it. Order out, or whatever.

This is the sauce that goes on all noodles—macaroni, spaghetti, linguine, whatever. You can call it pasta sauce if you want. But don't, if you want to be a goomba. No goomba calls it "pasta." That's a word they use in Italy. In America, it's a yuppie thing. Not for serious people. You say "macaroni" or "spaghetti." The end.

This is also the sauce that you use to build your lasagne, your manicotti, your sauce with meatballs, and a hundred other goomba meals. Get this right, and you got the whole thing.

For starters, just try making the sauce and putting it over noodles. Nothing fancy. No osso bucco yet. No baked rigatoni. Just macaroni. It should taste pretty good, just like that, with a little hard-crusted Italian bread, a little glass of Chianti, and a little Parmesan cheese grated over the top. If it doesn't, again, clear out. You got no business cooking this stuff—or even eating this stuff. Maybe you're WASP, God forbid. Eat a tuna fish sandwich.

SERVES 4

3 tablespoons olive oil
1 garlic clove, minced
1 28-ounce can tomatoes with their juices, diced
2 tablespoons chopped fresh basil or ½ teaspoon dried
¼ teaspoon salt
¼ teaspoon sugar
1 tablespoon olive oil
1 pound spaghetti

Heat 2 tablespoons of the oil in a saucepan over medium heat until it becomes fragrant. Mix the garlic with one teaspoon of water and carefully add this to the warm oil. Sauté the garlic and cook without browning it. Add the tomatoes, bring to a boil, then reduce the heat. Simmer for 10 minutes. Add the basil, sugar, and salt, and simmer 5 more minutes. Just before serving, blend in the last tablespoon of olive oil.

SPAGHETTI WITH SAUCE

Heat four quarts of water in a big pot. When it is boiling, add the spaghetti. Cook the noodles 11 to 13 minutes, depending on how al dente you want them to be. When they are right, drain the noodles in a colander. Drain them completely.

Serve the spaghetti in a big bowl, with the tomato sauce poured on top. Serve with bread and grated Italian Parmesan cheese. Salute!

Meat Sauce

The companion to the basic marinara sauce is the basic meat sauce, or Bolognese. Depending on where you grew up, where your mother grew up, and where her mother grew up, this sauce can be dark and meaty, light and tomatoey, or anything in between. Many a goomba argument has broken out over whose Bolognese is better. Many a goomba has vowed never to return to a restaurant where the Bolognese isn't the way he likes it. So you may have to experiment, if you don't have an Italian mother who already cooks it just right, before you find the recipe that's perfect for you. Use the recipe that follows as a suggestion. Add a little more tomato. Add a little less. Add oregano. Use less onion. Whatever!

Whenever I make this sauce, I make a big batch of it and refrigerate or even freeze some. That way, if company comes, if the card game goes late, if I'm too tired to go out, I already got dinner. Put this over pasta and it's a meal. Put it in lasagne for a meat lasagne. Cut a big hunk of Italian bread in half, add some Bolognese, and you got a sandwich. Add a meatball, you got a meatball sandwich. Add grilled Italian sausages, or roasted bell peppers . . . You get the point.

SERVES 4 TO 6

3 tablespoons butter
1 carrot, peeled and diced
1 small onion, diced
1 pound ground beef
1 pound ground veal (or ground pork)
1 teaspoon salt
½ teaspoon black pepper
2 tablespoons chopped parsley
1 cup whole milk
1 28-ounce can tomatoes with their juices

Melt the butter in a heavy, deep skillet. Sauté the carrot and onion over medium-high heat until they are soft, about 10 minutes. Add the ground meats, and the salt, pepper, and parsley. Cook for 5 minutes, breaking up the meat with a wooden spoon. When it is no longer pink, add the milk. Simmer until it has disappeared, and only the clear juice from the meat remains. Add the tomatoes. Lower the heat and simmer slowly for one hour.

Serve over noodles, with grated Parmesan cheese.

Lasagne Alla Nonna

Like I said, when I was a little boy, my grandmother was a famous cook in the neighborhood. She used to make a lasagne so good that the local Italian deli bought it from her and sold it as their own (right next to the eggplant—also hers). My grandmother would spend all day cooking—the sauce, the noodles—and she'd buy the whole neighborhood, too. Vegetables from here. Macaroni from there. Cheese from over there. She never, ever gave up the recipe for her lasagne. She'd say, "Oh, I use a little of this and a little of that." But she'd never say how much. She couldn't—it was her bread and butter, selling the lasagne to the deli, and she was afraid that if her recipe became public, someone else would start making the lasagne for the deli.

May she rest in peace, this is as close as I can come to her secret lasagne. You can't buy it, frozen, from the deli anymore. You gotta make it yourself, if you want lasagne like she used to make.

SERVES 6 TO 8

½ pound hot or sweet Italian sausage
1 pound lean ground beef
¼ cup chopped parsley
½ teaspoon salt
2 tablespoons olive oil
4 cups Tomato Sauce (page 186)
1 pound mozzarella cheese, grated
½ pound ricotta cheese
1 cup grated Parmesan cheese
1 pound lasagne noodles

Peel the casings off the sausage and mix with the ground beef and salt. Heat 1 tablespoon of the olive oil in a heavy skillet. Sauté the meat in the oil until browned and no longer pink, about 8 minutes. Remove the meat from the pan with a slotted spoon, and when it cools slightly pour off all the excess grease and liquid from the skillet.

Return the browned meat to the skillet, stir in the tomato sauce, and simmer over very low heat for 30 minutes. Meanwhile, combine the cheeses and mix them together with the parsley.

Bring 4 quarts of water to a boil. Cook the lasagne noodles until *al dente,* about 10 minutes, then drain them in a colander.

Preheat the oven to 350°F. Grease a 9- by 12-inch baking pan with the olive oil.

Spoon some of the tomato sauce into the bottom of the pan. Lay down one layer of the lasagne noodles. Lay down one quarter of the meat mixture. Spread one quarter of the cheese mixture on top. Repeat this three more times. For the top layer, cover the entire top with one final layer of cheese.

Cover the lasagne with foil, and bake at 350°F for 40 minutes. Remove the foil, and continue cooking for 15 more minutes, or until the cheese on top is browned and crispy. Let the lasagna stand for 10 minutes or more before serving.

Mangia!

Spaghetti with Meatballs

This is the classic goomba meal. It's almost a cliché. You think of an Italian. You imagine a fat guy, sitting in a restaurant, at a table with a red and white checkered tablecloth. On the table is a bottle of wine with straw wrapped around it. The guy's got his napkin stuck into his shirt collar. He's got a fork in one hand and a spoon in the other. What's he eating? Spaghetti and meatballs.

That's why Chef Boy-Ar-Dee has a job. That's where those horrible Spaghetti-Os come from. That's why every kid in America has eaten Italian food before he's five years old—even if he's Mexican or Chinese or Mormon or whatever. Everybody loves spaghetti and meatballs. Here's the simplest recipe I know for making this dish. It's fun to make and your kids can help and it tastes better than what you get in most restaurants.

SERVES 4 TO 6

½ pound ground beef
½ pound ground pork
½ pound ground veal
1 teaspoon salt
¼ cup chopped parsley
2 eggs, lightly beaten
¼ cup bread crumbs
1 tablespoon olive oil
4 cups Tomato Sauce (page 186)
1 pound spaghetti
½ cup grated Parmesan cheese

Combine all three kinds of ground meat in a mixing bowl with the salt and parsley. Then add the beaten eggs and the bread crumbs and mix thoroughly. On a piece of waxed paper, roll the meat into small balls—no bigger than an inch across.

Heat the olive oil in a heavy skillet. Brown the balls in the skillet, rolling them often to prevent burning and to cook on all sides. When they're browned, remove them from the pan and drain them on a paper towel. Then add them to your tomato sauce and simmer over low heat for 30 minutes.

Heat 4 quarts of water until boiling. Add the spaghetti noodles and cook until done, about 12 to 14 minutes. Drain the noodles in a colander. Serve the noodles and meatballs with sauce spooned over them. Sprinkle grated cheese on top.

Spaghetti Carbonara

This is almost like breakfast pasta. It's got eggs and bacon in it. Beautiful. It's also got cheese and onions and olive oil, so all the basic food groups are represented. This is a great thing to cook late at night, after a card game, after you've been out drinking, after you've done Scores and Goldfingers and you're still hungry. It's fast, it's filling, and it doesn't require a lot of concentration.

SERVES 4 TO 6

¼ pound bacon, cut into half-inch pieces
3 tablespoons olive oil
1 onion, diced
½ cup chopped parsley
1 cup ricotta cheese
½ pound prosciutto, sliced thin and chopped
2 egg yolks, lightly beaten
1 pound spaghetti
1 cup grated Parmesan cheese

Cook the bacon pieces in a heavy skillet over medium heat until they are brown. With a slotted spoon, remove the pieces and set aside. Add the olive oil to the pan with the bacon grease. Add the onions and cook over medium heat until they are tender, about 5 minutes. Put the bacon back on.

In a separate bowl, mix the parsley, ricotta, prosciutto, and egg yolks.

Heat 4 quarts of water until boiling.

Cook the spaghetti until it is the way you like it. Drain the noodles in a colander.

In a big serving bowl, toss the noodles with the parsley-cheese-prosciutto-egg mixture. Pour the onion-bacon mix on top. Mix.

Serve in individual bowls. Sprinkle the grated Parmesan on top.

Che bella pasta!

Frittata Italiana

If you want to have breakfast for breakfast, here's a nice way to start the day. You can do this on a Sunday morning, while your wife or your mother is thinking about the Sunday sauce. It's good served hot, right out of the oven, but it's also good served warm or room temperature, so it's good for entertaining. If you got a mob coming over, excuse the pun, you might make a couple of orders of this stuff and lay it out. Serve it with Italian sausages for a meatier meal.

SERVES 6

6 tablespoons olive oil
1 onion, diced
1 red bell pepper, cored, seeded, and diced
1 tomato, cored and diced
10 eggs
$\frac{1}{2}$ cup heavy cream
1 cup grated Parmesan cheese
1 teaspoon salt
$\frac{1}{2}$ teaspoon black pepper
$\frac{1}{4}$ teaspoon dried oregano
$\frac{1}{2}$ cup chopped parsley

Preheat your oven to 350°F. Heat the olive oil in a deep, heavy skillet that can go in the oven. Swirl the oil around so it coats the sides of the skillet. Sauté the onions and bell pepper until they are very soft, about 10 minutes. Add the tomato, and cook 2 minutes more. Meanwhile, beat the eggs slightly, and mix in the cream, cheese, salt, pepper, oregano, and parsley. Then add the egg mixture to the hot skillet.

Put the skillet in the oven and cook for 30 minutes, until the top is slightly browned. Remove and allow to cool for 10 minutes before serving.

Rigatoni Alla Vodka

Il Cortile has been serving since 1975 or something. I always have the rigatoni in the vodka sauce. Here's their recipe.

SERVES 4 TO 6

2 28-ounce cans tomatoes with their juices
3 tablespoons olive oil
3 garlic cloves
1 8-ounce can tomato paste
1 teaspoon dried oregano
½ teaspoon salt
½ teaspoon black pepper
½ cup vodka
1 cup heavy cream
1 pound rigatoni

Cut the hard ends of the tomatoes off and discard. Heat the olive oil in a wide, heavy pan. Sauté the garlic until it is soft but don't brown or burn it! Add the tomatoes, then add the tomato paste, oregano, salt, and pepper. Simmer over medium heat for 30 minutes, stirring occasionally, until the tomatoes begin to break down and turn into paste. Adjust the seasoning to taste. Stir in the vodka and simmer another 5 minutes. Stir in the cream and immediately remove from heat.

Heat 4 quarts of water in a big pot. When it's boiling, put in the rigatoni. Cook until the noodles are as soft or as firm as you like them. Drain completely in a colander. Portion out the noodles, and spoon out the sauce over them. You'll eat like it's your own funeral.

Chicken a la Rabbit Parmesi

My pet rabbit Sniffy became the main course for Mrs. Parmesi's Easter dinner when I was a child, so I can't recommend doing this recipe the way she did—with a real bunny. But it works great when you substitute chicken. Since I never had a pet chicken, I find this tastes beautiful and doesn't bring back any upsetting childhood memories.

SERVES 4

6 tablespoons (¾ stick) butter
4 strips bacon or ¼ pound sliced prosciutto
6 serving pieces of chicken (breasts and thighs) skin on
½ cup dry white wine
1 carrot, peeled and chopped
1 28-ounce can of tomatoes with their juices
¼ teaspoon salt
¼ teaspoon black pepper
1 tablespoon rubbed sage

Heat the butter in a wide, heavy pan. Add the bacon or the prosciutto and fry over medium-high heat until browned. Remove to a plate with a slotted spoon, then add the chicken pieces and cook until browned on all sides, about 15 minutes total. Remove the chicken pieces. Drain or skim all but about 1 tablespoon of the melted butter. Add the white wine, and the carrot, and cook until the wine is almost entirely evaporated. Toss in the tomatoes, then add the salt and pepper and sage. Bring almost to a simmer. Add the chicken pieces, cover and cook for 40 minutes on very low heat.

When ready to serve, remove the chicken pieces to a platter, and raise the heat to high. Cook the sauce, stirring constantly, until it is thick. Pour it over the chicken and serve.

Serve this with a simple side dish of noodles and cheese, with a nice Italian bread. Eat one for Sniffy.

Fusilli with Sausages and Peppers

Serve this with a nice green salad and a big Italian bread. Mangia tutti!

SERVES 4

- **1 pound hot Italian sausages**
- **1 tablespoon olive oil**
- **2 green bell peppers**
- **2 red bell peppers**
- **3 garlic cloves, minced**
- **1 onion, chopped**
- **1 28-ounce can of tomatoes, drained**
- **1 pound fusilli**

Cook the sausages in the olive oil in a wide, heavy pan turning to brown on all sides. Meanwhile, poke the green and red bell peppers with a fork and stick them under a very hot broiler. Roast them, turning them once every 3 minutes, until the outside skin is completely blackened. Remove the peppers with a pair of tongs, and stick them in a plastic bag. Close the bag and set it aside.

When the sausages are browned, remove them from the oil. Add the garlic and onion, and sauté slowly in the oil until very soft. When the peppers are cool, take them out of the plastic bag and peel off the blackened skin. Slice the peppers open and remove the core and seeds. Slice the peppers into strips, and add them to the pan with the garlic and onions. Add the tomatoes and simmer over medium heat for 20 minutes. Put the sausages back in and simmer 10 minutes more.

Bring 4 quarts of water to a boil in a big pot. Throw in the noodles, and stir. Cook until they are the consistency you like. Drain them completely in a colander. Portion out the noodles and spoon the sauce and sausages over them.

Osso Bucco a la Riv

*This is like the Cadillac of veal dishes—big, hearty, delicious, and
real easy to make. Don't tell anybody that, and if they don't know
how it's done they'll think you're a genius in the kitchen. The chef
at The Riviera used to make this special for me, even on days when
it wasn't on his menu. It was rich and full-bodied—just like some of
the high-rollers who ate it—and it made any meal feel like a
special occasion. Frank Sinatra, with whom every meal was a
special occasion, loved it. This makes a fine dinner for four,
especially if you serve it with a plate of pasta, or after a big bowl of
pasta fazool.*

SERVES 4

**2 veal shanks, cut into 3-inch lengths (have your
     butcher do this)**
½ cup flour
¼ cup olive oil
1 onion, thinly sliced
2 carrots, peeled and finely chopped
1 celery stalk, minced
1 bay leaf
½ cup dry white wine
1 28-ounce can of tomatoes with their juices
1 teaspoon grated lemon peel
2 tablespoons parsley, chopped
1 garlic clove, mashed

Dredge the shanks in the flour until they're powdered
white; knock off any excess. Heat the olive oil in a wide,
heavy pan. Brown the meat on all sides, cooking 5 to 7
minutes per side. Remove the meat from the pan.

In the same pan, sauté the onions, carrots, and celery until they turn soft, about 6 to 8 minutes. Add the bay leaf and the white wine, and bring it to a boil. Cook over high heat until the wine is almost all gone, then add the can of tomatoes. Place the veal pieces back into the pan, and cover the pot. Cook this on low heat, barely at a simmer, for 2 hours.

When you are almost ready to serve, transfer the meat to the serving platter, and add the lemon peel, parsley, and garlic to the sauce. Bring the sauce to a boil, and cook 5 minutes more. Serve this with a simple noodle with butter on the side, or a risotto, and a big Italian bread. You'll be dining in heaven, with The Chairman of the Board.

Spaghetti with Meatballs a la "Casino"

This is the classic. The goomba dinner. The basic goomba food. This is the one the Italian is eating in the cartoons and comic books. This is the meal that the stereotypical Italian eats—whether he's a goomba or a gangster or a prime minister. And it's the basic meal you need to cook if you want to run a real goomba kitchen. If you can make a basic plate of spaghetti and meatballs, you're basically done. You don't have to do anything else. You will, but you don't have to. You can eat this two times a day for the rest of your life and die happy. But don't. Do this, then learn how to do the other stuff, and then eat everything and die happy. After a long life of eating.

THE SAUCE

2 28-ounce cans of tomatoes with their juices
3 tablespoons olive oil
3 garlic cloves
1 8-ounce can of tomato sauce
1 teaspoon dried oregano
½ teaspoon salt
½ teaspoon black pepper
¼ teaspoon sugar

Open the tomatoes. Cut the hard ends of the tomatoes off and discard. Heat the olive oil in a wide, heavy pan. Sauté the garlic until it is soft—but don't brown or burn it! Add the tomatoes and the tomato sauce, and then the sugar and spices. Simmer over medium heat for 30 minutes, stirring occasionally, until the tomatoes begin to break down and turn into paste. Adjust spices to taste.

THE MEATBALLS

1 pound ground veal or pork or sirloin, or any 1-pound mix of those
4 tablespoons olive oil
1 garlic clove, minced
2 tablespoons parsley, chopped
½ teaspoon salt
½ teaspoon pepper
½ cup Parmesan cheese
1 egg, lightly beaten
¼ cup bread crumbs
1 pound spaghetti

Mix the meats together with the garlic, parsley, salt, pepper, Parmesan cheese, and beaten egg. Then sprinkle in the bread crumbs. Form meatballs no larger than one inch across. Heat the oil until it is hot, but not smoking. Gently place the meatballs into the pan, without crowding them together. (Most pans will do 10 to 12 at a time.) Slowly push the meatballs around, letting them brown gradually, and not letting them stick to the bottom. When they're brown all over, remove them to a plate lined with paper towels.

When the meatballs are done, put them into a saucepan with the tomato sauce. Simmer for 20 minutes. Heat 2 quarts of water in a large soup pot. Add the spaghetti noodles. Stir. Cook until they're the way you like them. Drain them completely into a colander. Serve the noodles with the sauce and meatballs on top. Eat a nice Italian bread with this. *Mangia!*

Chicken Piccata

This is a nice light meal for nights when you don't wanna eat a big veal or a big plate of pasta—or days when you want something good for lunch, or nights when you wanna eat a big veal, a big plate of pasta, and a little something extra. It cooks fast and easy, and doesn't take long to prepare.

SERVES 4

1 tablespoon olive oil
3 tablespoons butter
4 boneless, skinless chicken breast filets, pounded thin
flour
½ teaspoon salt
½ teaspoon black pepper
juice of 1 large lemon
1 tablespoon capers, drained

Melt 2 tablespoons of the butter and the olive oil in a heavy skillet. Dredge the pounded chicken breasts in flour you have spiced up with the salt and pepper. Brown the chicken breasts in the skillet until they are golden brown and crispy, at least 7 minutes a side. Remove the chicken to a plate. Add the last tablespoon of butter and when it melts, add the lemon juice. Cook the sauce over high heat until it thickens, then add the capers. Pour the sauce over the chicken breasts and serve immediately.

Roasted Peppers and Garlic

This is another great appetizer—good for snacks, good for antipasto, good on a sandwich, good on a salad, good all around. And I've never had store-bought that tasted better than homemade.

SERVES 4 TO 6

4 large red bell peppers
4 garlic cloves, mashed
½ cup olive oil
¼ teaspoon dried oregano
salt
pepper

Put the peppers under a hot broiler. Cook them until they are black all over—turning them periodically to blacken all sides. Remove them with tongs, and put them in a plastic bag. Twist the bag shut and let the peppers sit until they are cool. Peel and mash the garlic. Put it in a big bowl with the olive oil and the oregano and salt and pepper. When the peppers are cool, cut them in half, remove the cores and seeds, and peel the blackened skin off the outside. Slice the peppers into slivers, and put them into the oil. Let the peppers sit at least 30 minutes at room temperature before serving.

Pasta e Fagioli

This is one of the great goomba foods—goomba comfort food, if
you like. It's hearty and rich, and simple, and it has all the main
goomba food groups: meat, beans, macaroni. There's a thousand
ways to cook it. Some guys use beef stew meat instead of short ribs,
and some guys use soup bones. Sometimes it's very soupy, and other
times it's more like a stew. Either way, it's a delicious way to start a
meal, and it makes a very satisfying meal on its own.

SERVES 4 TO 6

¼ cup olive oil
1 pound beef short ribs
1 tablespoon dried basil or 2 tablespoons chopped
**   fresh**
2 garlic cloves, mashed
1 28-ounce can tomatoes with their juices, diced
1 pound dried cannelini beans or 2 16-ounce cans
**   cannelini beans (see Note)**
1 pound macaroni

NOTE: If you're using dried beans, soak them in cold water
overnight before beginning this recipe.

Heat the olive oil until it becomes fragrant. Add the short
ribs and brown well on all sides. Toss in the basil and the
garlic, and sauté for 2 minutes. Add the tomatoes and
simmer for 30 minutes.

Drain the beans and add them to the pot with enough
water to cover the short ribs by about two-thirds. Simmer
this over medium heat for 2 hours. Use a slotted spoon to
transfer about half the beans to a blender or a food

processor. Purée the beans until smooth. Return the puréed beans to the soup. In a separate pot of boiling water, cook the noodles until they are *al dente*. Save about 1 cup of the water you cooked the macaroni in, then drain the noodles. Add the macaroni to the soup. If it's too thick, add the cup of reserved water. Serve with grated Parmesan cheese and a nice Italian bread with a good crust. *Che bella pasta!*

MORE GOOMBA RECIPES

LIKE I SAID before, the food on the set of *The Sopranos* is always delicious. It has to be. With all those Italians running around, and all that goomba appetite at work, there'd be a riot if the food was lousy. There's always good food put out on tables for the actors and the crew to eat during their breaks. And there's always something extremely good for the sit-down meals.

One of the catering companies that does *Sopranos* food is Premiere Caterers from New Jersey. They really know their stuff. Here's a few recipes they gave me, so I could cook the way they cook when I'm not working.

Smothered New York Sirloin Steak

This dish puts the "sir" back in "sirloin"; it really makes a great meal. And it's easy as hell to put together. You serve it with a baked potato, a little red wine, a nice Italian bread . . . Bad-a-bing!

SERVES 4

4 8-ounce New York strip steaks
2 tablespoons black pepper
3 teaspoons salt
6 tablespoons (¾ stick) butter
½ cup dry red wine
1 large onion, sliced
2 garlic cloves, minced
1 cup heavy cream

Season the steaks with the salt and pepper. Melt the butter in a large, heavy skillet over medium-high heat until it sizzles. Add the steaks and cook for 3 to 5 minutes on each side—depending on how well done you like your meat. Transfer the steaks to a platter and keep warm.

Pour the wine into the skillet and boil over high heat for a minute or so, scraping the brown bits up with a wooden spoon. Toss in the onion and the garlic, and cook for a minute or two. Add the heavy cream, and simmer for 6 minutes more. Return the steaks to the pan and heat in the sauce for 2 minutes, turning once. Serve.

Always Perfect Pepper Shrimp Scampi

This makes a terrific lunch, a terrific snack, a terrific appetizer, and a terrific light dinner. You can't miss with this one. And the ladies love it—they think it's fancy food. Don't tell 'em how easy it is to cook. Just serve it and watch their reaction. Single guys: If you serve this to your date and can't score . . . fuhgeddaboudit. She's the wrong girl for you.

SERVES 4 TO 6 AS AN APPETIZER; 2 OR 3 AS AN ENTREE

1 pound extra-large shrimp, peeled and deveined
3 tablespoons butter
4 garlic cloves, minced
⅓ cup chopped Italian parsley
½ cup dry white wine
1 teaspoon salt
1 teaspoon black pepper
1 teaspoon hot red pepper flakes

Melt the butter in a large skillet. Add the shrimp and sauté over high heat for 6 minutes, until almost cooked. Add the garlic and sauté for another minute. Stir in the white wine and cook for 30 seconds or so, scraping the bottom of the pan. Add the salt, pepper, and hot pepper flakes, and continue to cook just until the shrimp are completely opaque, another minute or so. Sprinkle with the parsley. Serve over a bed of steamed rice as a main course or side dish, or on their own as appetizers.

Chicken Marsala a la Minute

This is another fancy-looking dish, an Italian classic that's very easy to cook. It's great date food—women love it—and it's also a very manly meal at the same time. It only takes about ten minutes to cook, and hardly more time than that to prepare, so dig in. If you can make this, you're a made man—that is, you could qualify to be a chef in any neighborhood Italian restaurant.

SERVES 6

6 boneless, skinless chicken breasts
2 cups all-purpose flour
1 teaspoon salt
1 teaspoon black pepper
1 tablespoon Cream of Wheat
3 tablespoons butter
2 cups mushrooms, sliced
1 cup Marsala wine
2 cups heavy cream
egg noodles for 4

Pound the chicken breasts a few times on each side until they are slightly flattened. Mix the flour, salt, pepper, and Cream of Wheat in a shallow dish. Dredge the chicken in the flour mixture.

Melt the butter in a large skillet over medium-high heat until it is sizzling. Sauté the chicken breasts until golden on both sides, about 10 minutes. Add the remaining butter, the mushrooms, and the Marsala and cook over high heat for 4 minutes. Stir in the heavy cream, reduce the heat to a rapid simmer and cook 6 minutes more. Serve over a bed of egg noodles. *Buono appetito!*

~ ~ ~

The father of a friend of mine was talking to me recently about how he grew up with food, and with the traditions of food. He remembers going to his grandfather's house—the grandfather who had come from Italy, and who spoke very little English, and who was the center of the family life—for all the holiday meals. He said,

> I remember thinking all my amerigan friends and classmates only ate turkey on Thanksgiving or Christmas. Or rather that they ate only turkey with stuffing, mashed potatoes, and cranberry sauce. Now, we Italians, we also had turkey with stuffing, mashed potatoes, and cranberry sauce—but only after we had finished the antipasto, soup, lasagne, meatballs, salad, and whatever else Mama thought might be appropriate for that particular holiday. The turkey was always accompanied by a roast of some kind (just in case somebody walked in who didn't like turkey) and was followed by an assortment of fruits, nuts, pastries, cakes, and, of course, homemade cookies. No holiday was complete without some home baking.

Just like in my house, and in every goomba house, my friend remembers Sunday being the big day of the week. There was a lot to eat in his house, because his family was religious—and everyone had to fast in the morning before taking communion! They'd go off to Mass hungry. "But we knew," he told me,

when we got home we'd find hot meatballs frying. In the morning you'd wake up to the smell of garlic and onions frying in olive oil. As you laid in bed, you could hear the hiss as tomatoes were dropped into a pan. Sunday we always had gravy (the amerigans *called it "sauce") and a macaroni (they called it "pasta"). After church, nothing tastes better than newly fried meatballs and crisp bread dipped in the gravy.*

What a memory! Why does a guy like that remember lying in bed hearing the sound of tomatoes cooking? Probably because he wakes up every Sunday, even today, with the same sound in his ears. Only now it's not someone cooking at his Mama's house, or his grandfather's house, it's his wife or his daughter cooking in *his* house! It's tradition, goombas and food.

AFTERWORD

By now I hope I've shown you that a little bit of goomba can go a long way toward getting a guy the good things in life. I'm living proof of that. I arrived in Las Vegas with a couple hundred bucks in my pocket, with no job, no place to stay, no contacts, and no guarantees. Ten years later, I was entertainment director of The Riviera Hotel. And a few years after that, I'm showing up on TV and movies all over the place.

A goomba like me. Go figure.

So now that I've more or less made it, does that mean I'll be leaving my goomba roots behind? Moving to Scarsdale or Scottsdale or some other place and renaming my kids Tyler and Lane? What do you think? It's goomba that's gotten me this far and I'm sticking with it. Let me tell you why.

Back when I first moved to Vegas, I got a job as a bouncer at this nightclub called Jubilation. It was owned by Paul Anka, and it was where all the heavy players hung out in the late 1970s. From there I got a job doing security at another club, where the heavy players hung out in the early 1980s. From there, I got a similar job someplace else. I worked hard. I got to know everybody who was anybody. When a job opened up at the Riviera, for a maitre d' at the comedy club, this guy I knew asked me to take it. He wanted to open up an Improv Club, just like the one in Los Angeles. I said yes. Not too long after that, there was a shake-up in management at The Riv, and I wound up running the front of the house.

They asked me to be entertainment director. I had no idea what that meant. They gave me a secretary and an office. I went out and bought five new suits. I had no clue what I was supposed to do. I didn't know any agents, any managers, any talent scouts. I didn't know anyone in the business. I jumped in and worked that job for five years.

And it was all great stuff for the goomba. The comedy club was wonderful. I gave a lot of guys their first shot at playing a big room. I booked Ray Romano, and Pauly Shore, and Paul Rodriguez. I booked Drew Carey for his first big room show. I brought in Chris Rock, and Rosie O'Donnell, and Ellen De Generes, and Sinbad.

Some of them were wonderful. Some of them were just weird. I met Tony Bennett. What a great guy! A beautiful guy—but a weird guy. He invited us over. We came and sat down at his table. He says hello, and then he doesn't say another word. All he does is tap his spoon in time with the music. Everybody else is talking. Tony is just smiling, and tapping his spoon. Never said a word.

Some of them were difficult to work with. Pauly Shore was one of them. Soupy Sales, too. Soupy Sales! He was my childhood idol. But he was so awful to work with. He had this enormous ego, and he was incredibly demanding and abusive to my employees. He got angry when he checked in to the hotel and no one recognized him. Then he got a car and drove down the Strip and looked at the hotel marquees. He saw Wayne Newton's name, and Tom Jones' name. He came back and said, "There's no one in town. I'm the biggest name in town!" I had to scream at him on the phone. Me, screaming at Soupy Sales! It was like screaming at Bozo the Clown. Ridiculous!

Pauly Shore was impossible, too. And Gabe Kaplan. They were both incredible cheapskates. Gabe Kaplan tried to walk out on a check. I was the bouncer then. I had to chase him down and take him back into the club. I said to him, "We can do this the easy way, or the hard way." We did it the easy way. With Pauly Shore, it was even worse. He was headlining the big room at The

Riv. He's the main act. So, we *know* who he is, right? But he's ordering food and drinks and stuff, and he's signing someone else's name and room number. He's on a per diem, and he's getting a big salary, and he's trying to stiff us on a check for a couple of cocktails.

But I also worked with David Spade, who was wonderful. And Louie Anderson, who was just a big, sweet guy. I booked Bobby Vinton and Frankie Avalon, and Brian Wilson and the Beach Boys—and they were all terrific. I booked Dennis Leary and Kevin James and Keenan Ivory Wayans and Drew Carey. All terrific guys.

I was polite and professional with every one of those guys, no matter how big or little they were. That's a goomba thing. A goomba is never rude to somebody for no reason. And I was always firm with them no matter how big a pain in the neck they were. A goomba never kisses anyone's ass for any reason—and especially not because they're famous or because they think they're important. You treat everybody the same.

I still live by that code and think the world would be a better place if more people did. But hey, that's just one goomba's opinion. I rest my case.

What, you thought *Sopranos* star Steven
Schirripa was finished wising you up? In his
new book, *The Goomba's Book of Love,* he helps
every goomba, non-goomba, goombette, and
goomba-wannabe figure out the basics and
some of the finer points of goomba *amore*.

1-4000-5089-8
$23.00 hardcover

CLARKSON POTTER/PUBLISHERS

Available October 2003, wherever books are sold.

The
GOOMBA'S
Book of *Love*

Steven R. Schirripa

and

CHARLES FLEMING

Authors of the
NATIONAL BESTSELLER
A Goomba's Guide to Life

$\mathcal{T}$he Goomba is a lovin' man. The one thing he understands, better than anything else in the world except for maybe food, is love. The goomba is practically made of love. His entire life is about love—family love, romantic love, brotherly love, motherly love. He loves his wife—and his *goomar*. He loves his children and his parents. He loves his car and his clothes. He loves to eat and drink and fool around. As a friend, as a father, as a husband, as a lover, the goomba is a big, bubbling, oozing, overflowing . . . well, you get the idea. The goomba is just full of love.

The non-goombas out there may not understand this. They look at the average goomba and what do they see? A big guy, a big appetite, a lot of noise, a certain level of violence, all of it flavored with garlic and tomato sauce on a bed of macaroni. They're missing the point. All that bigness—the big appetite, the big noise and yelling, the big food—that's all about love, too.

If you missed my first book, *A Goomba's Guide to Life,* this might be confusing. You might not even know what a "goomba" is. You're thinking: wise guy, good-fella, mobbed up, made man, mafia don, whatever. You might think "goomba" is an insult, like "greaseball" or "guinea" or "wop." That ain't it.

Goomba is a term of endearment. It's used to describe an Italian-American man of a certain type. He's probably from the East Coast. He's probably third or fourth generation American. He's got a name that ends in a vowel. He works a blue-collar job. He's loyal, stubborn, and patriotic. He idolizes Frank Sinatra. He drives a Cadillac or a Camaro. He's a flashy dresser, even when he's wearing nothing but a track suit and a tasteful layer of gold chains. The goomba isn't a college professor, but he's no dummy either.

If you live in New York, New Jersey, or Nevada, you've probably seen lots of goombas out and about.

You've probably seen the goomba in action. Because they got a lot of goombas there, and there's a lot of action. The average goomba is always looking for love, one way or another. He might be looking for the love of his life, for the girl he's going to make his wife. He might already be married, in which case he's looking for a *goomar* for the time when he's not with his wife. He might just be looking for sex. But he's always looking.

He's probably not traveling alone. The goomba don't work alone. He's in a group of three or four guys, or more. They're out having a drink, having a meal, watching the game, laying down a few bets or whatever. But out of the corner of their eyes, they're also checking out the broads. This is one of the defining characteristics of the goomba. They are always, no matter what else they're doing, checking out the broads. A goomba could be on his deathbed, but I guarantee you he's looking at the nurse and thinking, "I could nail her." He could be in court staring at life-without-possibility, but you just know he's thinking, "She's not bad looking—for a judge. I wonder if she wears panties under that robe." When the goomba gets to heaven, the first thing he says to St. Peter is, "So, how's the action around here?"

If you're not from one of those goomba capitals, or you're not sure whether the guys you're looking at are true goombas, pay attention to the way they talk. Goombas say, and don't say, certain things.

Things you'll always hear a goomba say:

"Yo, Vinnie!"

"I made him an offer he couldn't refuse."

"Let's eat."

On the other hand, there's things that a goomba just couldn't say.

Things you'll never hear a goomba say:

"Checkmate."

"Two Pink Ladys for me and my friend, bartender."

"Where the fuck did I put my cowboy hat?"

If you're still confused about what is and what is not a goomba, here's a little refresher course.

You might be a goomba if:

You've ever eaten a sandwich on the toilet.

You own underwear that says "Home of the Whopper"
     on it.

The photo in your high school yearbook was your mug shot.

You own a VCR, a CD player, and a DVD player, but you've never been in a store that sells these items.

Your mother's apartment has a framed picture of Frank Sinatra on the wall, next to a framed picture of Jesus Christ.

You can't be a goomba if:

You pay taxes.

You vote.

You listen to country music.

You shop at Old Navy.

You ever sat in the cheap seats.

Still confused? Here are some more guidelines.

You're probably not a goomba if:

You've ever said, "Pass the Velveeta."

You've ever said, "Is Oprah on yet?"

You knit.

You know anyone who knits.

You ever said to your wife, "Sit down and let *me* do the dishes."

On the other hand, you're *definitely* a goomba if:

You'd rather starve than eat a Domino's pizza.

You'd rather starve than eat anything made by Ragu.

You'd rather starve than eat anything served at The Olive
Garden.

You have a middle name that starts with "The."

You know a guy who knows a guy.

Above all, the goomba is passionate. Everything he
does—whether it's cooking dinner, chasing women, or
placing a bet with his bookie—he does with feeling. He's
quick to fight, quick to forgive, and just as quick to fall
in love.

How do I know? I'm a goomba! I grew up surrounded by goombas. All my best friends are goombas.
All my heroes are goombas.

So believe me when I tell you this: Boil it all down,
and the bottom line on the goomba is . . . love.

Consider *The Godfather*. Look at the love in that family. Everything that happens in that story is about love—
Don Corleone's love for his sons, Michael's love for his
father, and everybody's love for power and money.

Look at *The Sopranos*. What was that show really
about? Love! The love of family and family honor.
Carmela's love for Tony. Tony's love for Carmela. And
everybody's love for baked ziti and gabagool.

Look at the lyrics to the famous song: "When the moon hits your eye, like a big pizza pie . . . that's *amore.*" It's practically the goomba national anthem, as sung by that great goomba Dean Martin (real name, Dino Crocetti), and what's it called? *"Amore"!* Again with the love!

Here's the average goomba: He's got a big family, brothers and sisters, cousins and aunts and uncles, a bunch of kids, a wife, and two or maybe three girlfriends on the side. He needs a lot of love! Because he's got a lot of love to give.

He expresses it in all kinds of ways. The loving goomba father says things to his kids, like

"Finish your dinner, or there'll be no gun for Christmas."

"Never mind whose bike it is. Just enjoy it."

"If your buddy Tony shot someone and threw him off a bridge, I suppose you'd do that, too?"

The loving goomba boyfriend does crazy things when he's in love, like stealing flowers from the cemetery, or actually obeying the restraining order. The loving goomba husband never lets his wife catch him cheating on her with his girlfriend—because that would hurt her feelings. The really loving goomba husband buys a diamond ring for his wife that's even bigger than the one he bought for himself.

In my first book, *A Goomba's Guide to Life,* I explained how to live like a guy from the neighborhood—how to walk, talk, and dress like a goomba, how to tip a maitre d', how to behave at a funeral, how to cook a plate of macaroni. But I think maybe the best lesson you can take away from any goomba is how to *love* like a guy from the neighborhood—how to be the best goomba boyfriend, husband, parent, son, or friend you can be.

Is goomba love really so different from, say, Puerto Rican love, or suburban love, or cowboy love? You bet.

To the non-goomba, *everything* about goomba love is probably going to be confusing. Because, vice versa, everything about non-goomba love is confusing to the goomba.

For example, the personal ads. No goomba would ever try and meet a girl through the personal ads. If you're a goomba, you meet a girl through people you know. You have to be able to check her out. You have to know about her family. For most goombas, this is easy.

Most goombas wind up marrying girls they've known for years—neighborhood girls, where you know their brothers and their parents and all their friends before you even go out.

With the personals, what is that? It's like buying a used car. From a crooked dealer. Because you know no one is telling the truth in those ads. I see some of the ones they have today and I have to laugh. They have these categories: "Celebrity I Resemble Most." Apparently all men resemble Harrison Ford, Ben Affleck, or Jerry Seinfeld, and all women resemble Cameron Diaz, Jennifer Lopez, or Julia Roberts. Then you look at the pictures next to the ads, and you think, "He looks like Quasimodo. She looks like Moby Dick."

If the goomba ran an ad, the answers would be a little different:

> Occupation: I'm in the construction and sanitation business.
> Celebrity I Resemble Most: Half Robert De Niro, half
>   Al Pacino. Some Ben Affleck.
> Last Great Book I Read: *Bookmaking for Dummies.*
> In My Bedroom You'll Find: One Glock, one baseball bat, a
>   half-empty jar of Vaseline, cannoli crumbs, and me with
>   a hard-on, baby!

Five Items I Can't Live Without: Garlic, my Cadillac, my
bookie's cell phone number, my gold chains, and
crushed red pepper.

Who would answer an ad like that? Actually, a lot of
goombettes. They know a goomba when they see one,
and they like what they see.

And they're not wrong. Because a goomba in love is
a powerful force. The way he loves his mother, his kids,
his women—the wife and anyone else he may be doing
on the side—the way he loves his capacola sandwich—
it's something no one should get in the way of. It's a
beautiful thing.

The following chapters will show you how to make
amore the goomba way. When you're done, you'll be
like Barry White—deep, wide, and full of love—but
probably still white.

Love comes in many forms. Especially for the
goomba, who is so full of love. It's the love of friends
and family, the love of food and sex, the love of the
good things in life. For a goomba, love—not money,
not fame—is the most powerful force in nature.